WITCHCRAFT
—AND—
DEMONOLOGY

WITCHCRAFT
— A N D —
DEMONOLOGY

FRANCIS X. KING

CRESCENT BOOKS
New York

FOREWORD

Anyone who writes of subjects such as witchcraft, demonology and black magic is inevitably asked 'Do you believe in all that'?

It is a question I have always found it impossible to answer with an unqualified yes or no.

I do, of course, believe in the existence of people living at the present day who regard themselves as witches – indeed I know some of them. I also believe these people, or at least most of them, to be sincere, to have themselves done those things which they claim to have done. Whether or not some of them also possess supernormal powers is for me an open question. I am sure, however, that they have a knowledge of complex techniques involving ritual and the use of creative fantasy which can result in remarkable transformations of consciousness.

As far as witchcraft in past centuries is concerned, I do not accept that there was ever a large scale witch cult of either the sort believed in by the late Montague Summers, a conspiracy led by Satan, or a widespread survival of an ancient fertility religion. I am sure, however, that there have always been a number of people, either working individually or in small groups, who have practised witchcraft and magic, both black and white.

And demons? Yes, I believe in them – but I am not sure whether they are objective beings or merely personifications of the darkness and evil which lurk, usually below the levels of consciousness, in the minds of each and every one of us, even the most saintly.

Francis X. King

First published in 1987 by
The Hamlyn Publishing Group Limited

© Copyright The Hamlyn
Publishing Group Limited 1987

This 1991 edition published by Crescent Books
distributed by Outlet Book Company, Inc,. a Random
House Company, 225 Park Avenue South, New York,
New York 10003

ISBN 0-517-05921-5

Printed and bound in Hong Kong

Endpapers: 17th-century engraving of Walpurgis Night. Bibliothèque des Arts Décoratifs/Jean Loup-Charmet.

Page 5: Temptation of St Anthony from the Isenheim Altarpiece. Unterlinden Museum, Colmar/Giraudon.

Title Page: The Witch by David Ryckaert. Kunsthistorisches Museum, Vienna/The Aldus Archive/BPCC.

CONTENTS

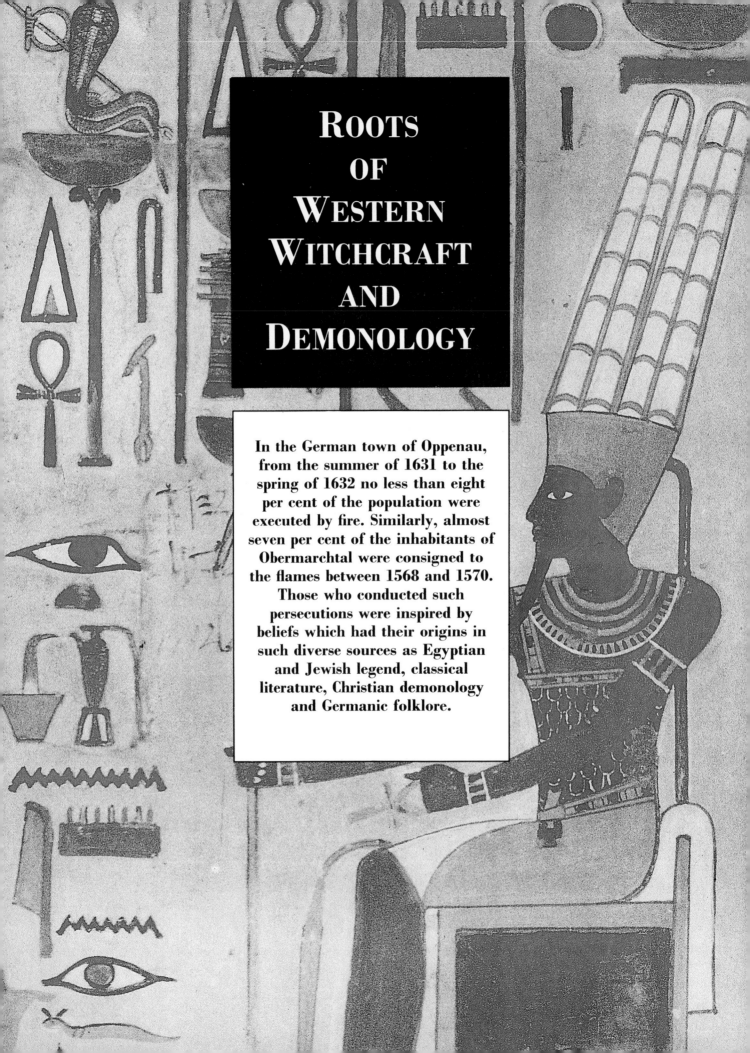

ROOTS
OF
WESTERN
WITCHCRAFT
AND
DEMONOLOGY

In the German town of Oppenau, from the summer of 1631 to the spring of 1632 no less than eight per cent of the population were executed by fire. Similarly, almost seven per cent of the inhabitants of Obermarchtal were consigned to the flames between 1568 and 1570. Those who conducted such persecutions were inspired by beliefs which had their origins in such diverse sources as Egyptian and Jewish legend, classical literature, Christian demonology and Germanic folklore.

THE POWERS OF DARKNESS

Those who toiled to build Stonehenge almost certainly thought of themselves as erecting a defence against those powers of darkness which then as now, mankind has always feared.

The existence of malignant supernatural forces which are hostile to humanity and are responsible for ill fortune, disease, sterility and death is a feature of every set of primitive beliefs. So strongly has this belief been held that in some cultures which survived into the present century it was held that there was no such thing as a natural death. If someone fell ill or died, if a hunter was killed by a wild animal, or if a child stumbled, fell, and suffered a fatal concussion, supernatural factors were believed to have been involved.

Such factors might be totally nonhuman: perhaps a god, or the spirit of a tree which had objected to some accidental act of disrespect, or a demon of the night. More commonly it was thought that some person who was possessed of baneful powers, a sorcerer or a witch, had been responsible for the 'natural' death.

Anthropologists have drawn a distinction between sorcery and witchcraft. The former they define as a body of technical knowledge concerning the occult powers and use of natural substances or things, such as a particular herb, the bone of an animal, or a curiously shaped stone. The latter is used for the employment of the inner powers of an individual, which is usually destructive.

Murder by magic

On this definition the sorcerer would kill enemies by the mechanical manipulation of matter, in the form of a wax image for example, while muttering spells or invoking demons. The witch, however, would achieve the same ends by a simple curse which directed the inner power against opponents.

The distinction is, no doubt, a useful one, but in practice sorcery and witchcraft are rarely found in total isolation from each other. The witch of aboriginal Australian folklore, the individual whose glance would suffice to kill a baby suckling at its mother's breast, was also held capable of such sorcery as 'pointing the bone', i.e., manipulating a bone, while uttering magical formulae in order to inflict a slow but certain death upon an enemy.

Dark divinities

In Europe, from classical times until the present day, there has been a similar blurring between witchcraft, sorcery and evocatory ceremonial magic, the latter being the use of ceremony in order to obtain the services of spirits for both good and evil purposes. Thus, in ancient Greece, the three were all reputed to be practised by the same individuals. Such a person could, so it was believed, either kill or induce burning sexual desire by a look, use philtres, potions or spells to achieve the same ends, or evoke the dark gods and goddesses of the underworld to visible appearance.

Two thousand years later, and three thousand miles away, a similar blurring of the boundaries between sorcery, witchcraft and ceremonial magic can be discerned in some of the evidence given in the course of the witchcraft trials of 17th-century New England. The New England witches could kill their neighbours' pigs or blast their crops by a malignant wish, but they also used sorcery involving material substances and employed unholy ceremony for the purpose of summoning the imps of hell to their service.

EGYPTIAN SORCERY

There is a shop in New York which sells what are called 'love spell kits'. Each kit is made up of an instructional leaflet, which includes the words of a magic spell, a bag of a herb believed to have occult properties concerned with human sexuality, and two small rag dolls.

The purchaser is instructed to take the dolls and, after stuffing them with the herb, tie them together in a manner suggestive of physical lovemaking. A ritual is then performed with the intention of bringing together the couple with whom the purchaser has chosen to identify the dolls in his mind.

The kits may, or may not, be effective – certainly the owner of the shop which sells them seems to get very few complaints from dissatisfied customers. However, what is an undoubted fact is that those who experiment with them are employing 'image magic', perhaps the

Like Thoth, god of learning, and the demon Typhon-Set, the favours of the dog-headed god, Anubis, were much sought after by the Graeco-Egyptian magicians of classical times.

most ancient of the techniques traditionally associated with witchcraft and sorcery and one which was commonly used in ancient Egypt.

Water magic

A very early Egyptian story, believed to date from before 3000 BC, tells of a certain Abaaner, an official high in the Pharaoh's favour who was also skilled in image magic. Abaaner discovered that his wife had been unfaithful with a soldier, so he made a small wax image of a crocodile, only seven hands' breadth in length, and muttered a spell over it. When the soldier came down to bathe in the Nile a servant, following Abaaner's instructions, hurled the model into the river.

ensured that his own ships 'should vanquish the enemy and sink his ships to the bottom of the bowl, as simultaneously did his real ships sink the enemy's craft in the depths of the sea'.

Monster god of sorcery

The god to whom Egyptian black magicians in the time of Nectanebus were reputed to be indebted for their sinister knowledge of the techniques of sorcery was Set. He has been identified with Satan although, in fact, the latter name is derived from the Hebrew, not Egyptian.

Originally, Set seems to have been the god of a southern people who had been conquered by northern Egypt at a very early date. At first he seems to have been

Protective charms and amulets, consecrated and endowed with mystic powers by priests and sorcerers, were prized greatly in ancient Egypt. This one was designed to protect against harmful creatures.

It immediately turned into a full-sized living creature, seized the soldier in its jaws and carried him to the bottom of the river.

Tales of image magic recur throughout the history of ancient Egypt and it is fitting that Nectanebus, the country's last native ruler until modern times, was reputed to be adept at this sinister art, applying it even to naval warfare. Clad in the robes of an enchanter, Nectanebus would make small wooden models of his ships and those of his opponents and float them, complete with crews of tiny dolls, in a huge bowl of water. He would intone words of power and then, said a Greek writer, 'the dolls would come to life and the ships engage in battle'. By judicious interference Nectanebus

venerated by both conquerors and conquered, but as the centuries went by he acquired an increasingly sinister reputation. He was regarded as the murderer of the fertility god, Osiris, as the treacherous warrior who had blinded Horus, the Egyptian war god, and as favouring the cause of Assyria, Persia and other foreign invaders.

By the time of Nectanebus, Set had become identified with Typhon, the monster-god of Greek mythology, and as Set-Typhon he was an important figure in late magical papyri. In the spells given in these, he is shown in a manner remarkably similar to that in which the Devil allegedly was presented by the witches of a later age.

. . . you and your associates have denied God . . . you have worshipped . . . the Prince of Devils in the shape of a deformed and hideous black goat . . . and did call upon him . . . and invoke his help . . .

So, in part, ran an accusation of witchcraft made in 16th-century Avignon. The 'Prince of Devils' is, of course, usually called Satan or Lucifer and both these names have their origin in the Old Testament and Jewish legend.

'Satan' is derived from a Hebrew word meaning adversary, and is therefore applicable to the Devil, opponent of light and good, but Lucifer means 'light-bearer'; it was one of the Latin names of the morning star, and so seems an odd name for the prince of darkness.

In ancient Israel, however, the morning star had a sinister reputation, being identified with the archangel who, rebelliously, had endeavoured to become God's equal. 'How art thou fallen from heaven, O morning star' proclaimed the prophet Isaiah, who went on to foretell that it would be brought down 'to the uttermost parts of the pit of hell'.

Lucifer and his watchers

In Latin translations of Isaiah, the Hebrew words meaning 'morning star' were rendered as Lucifer. In time Lucifer, the rebellious angel of the morning star, became identified with Satan, the eternal adversary. Lucifer, it was said, had been the archangel's only name before his rebellion; afterwards he was also Satan, God's opponent.

The story of Lucifer's fall from heaven became merged with elements derived from two other strands

Lucifer and those angels who had followed him in his revolt against the Almighty descend into the place set apart for them – Pandemonium.

A certain sympathy for Satan can be discerned perhaps in William Blake's depiction of him as a supernatural rabble-rouser addressing his fellow rebels.

At the time of the great European witch persecutions, during the period 1450–1650, all these strands of Jewish legend had been woven into one body of belief. Lucifer, the archangel of the morning star, had rebelled against God and become Satan who, as the serpent, had been responsible for the sin of Eve and the fall of man. His demon servants were the Watchers, who still desired the daughters of men and slaked their lusts at the Witches' Sabbath. Those human beings who attended such Sabbaths were Satan's servants and allies and merited the axe, the rope, and the stake, both for their worship of the Devil and for their participation in unholy rites involving murder, cannibalism and perverted sexuality.

Almost 2,000 years earlier very similar crimes had been committed allegedly by the devotees of Hecate, dark queen of Hell and goddess of the witches of Thessaly.

Some occultists have interpreted Bosch's paintings as indications that he possessed the power of 'astral vision'; that with his inner eye he directly perceived the realms of Satan.

of Jewish legend, both derived from the Book of Genesis. The first of these concerned demons known as the Watchers, while the second was derived from the story of Eve's temptation by the serpent.

Genesis refers to beings called 'the sons of God' who took human wives, fathered children, and spread evil throughout the earth. By the early centuries BC, this reference had been evolved into a very complex story. The 'sons of God', said the *Book of Enoch*, which was written about 100 BC, were 200 angels of the order of Watchers (whose proper task was to watch over humanity). They came to earth, lusted sinfully after women, and taught mankind the evil arts of war, astrology and magic. As a result of these sins they fell like Satan and became his subjects, devoting themselves to the corruption and enslavement of men and women.

The serpent of desire

Originally, the serpent of Genesis, Eve's tempter, had been regarded as a being in its own right, not a manifestation of the adversary. However, by the early centuries AD, most Jewish rabbis had come to believe that the serpent was an incarnation of Satan and that he had been motivated by a sexual desire for Eve.

William Blake's depiction of the tripke lunar aspects of Hecate, Queen of Hades, drinker of blood, ruler of night and goddess of the witches of Thessaly.

Hellish, Earthly and Heavenly . . . goddess of the crossroads, guiding light, Queen of Night, enemy of the sun, friend and companion of darkness; you who rejoice . . . to see blood flow; you who wander amidst the tombs in the hours of darkness, thirsty for blood and the terror of mortals; Gorgo, Mormo, moon of a thousand shifting forms . . .

So ran an ancient invocation of Hecate, the triple-headed demon goddess whom the ancient Greeks believed to be the queen of darkness, death, perverse sexuality and, above all, witchcraft.

Most of the malignant immortals of Greek mythology and folklore were female and many of them were looked upon as being particular aspects of Hecate. Thus, in the invocation quoted above the witch-goddess was hailed as 'Gorgo', and also 'Mormo'. The second of these names was that of a cannibalistic demon reputed to eat the souls of young children, but the first, Gorgo, was one of the names of Medusa, a gorgon whose face was that of a lovely woman but whose scalp was covered with writhing and venomous snakes. Serpents were sacred to Hecate, as were all carrion eaters.

The rituals used in ancient Greece for the purpose of calling the dark goddess of witchcraft to visible appearance bear some resemblance to those described in the evidence given at the witch trials almost 2,000 years later. Thus, in one classical version of the story of the Argonauts, the hero Jason is told by the witch Medea that to encounter the 'triple-headed, excrement-eating virgin . . . of the Underworld' he must sacrifice a sheep at midnight, pray to Hecate, pour honey upon the ground and walk away without looking behind him. Jason performed the rite and was rewarded by a vision of the witch-queen who appeared crowned with writh-

Cerberus the dog-demon of Hades, the underworld of classical mythology, was the archetype of the dogs of hell, the companions of Hecate, goddess of witchcraft.

ing serpents, with the dogs of hell fawning at her feet – dogs and the flesh of dogs were sacred to Hecate – and illuminated by the red glare of a thousand flaring torches.

Drawing down the moon

Hecate's most devoted servants were held to be the witches of Thessaly, a part of northern Greece on the borders of Macedonia, which in classical times had the reputation of being the home of sorcery and black magic. These women were suspected of having the power to 'draw down the moon' (that is, being able to employ the evil and averse aspects of lunar forces), the ability to transform themselves into birds and animals, and a sinister understanding of both poisonous and aphrodisiac herbs. They were also credited with the possession of insatiable sexual appetites.

Gnawers of the dead

Apuleius, a classical author who himself once stood trial on a charge of black magic, provided a description of the contents of a Thessalonian witch's den. It contained incenses, metal discs engraved with occult signs, the beaks and claws of birds of ill omen, various pieces of human flesh, notably the noses of victims of crucifixion, small vials of blood taken from the witch's murdered victims, and the skulls of criminals 'who had been thrown to wild beasts'.

The Thessalonian witches were believed to eat human flesh, as well as to use it ritually and in the manufacture of magic philtres of love and death. In some parts of Greece, corpse watchers were employed with the object of preventing these creatures from gnawing at the bodies of the newly dead.

It will be remembered that one of the epithets applied to Hecate was 'excrement-eating' and, accord-

ing to Greek folklore, the black goddess's worshippers were almost as fascinated by excreta as they were by corpses. One classical account of an attack on a man by Thessalonian witches records that they 'pissed long and vigorously on his face'. Similar scatological pursuits were indulged in by some of the cultists who practised their black arts in Rome and its Italian provinces.

Medea, enchantress of the legendary Jason who sailed in search of the Golden Fleece, rejuvenating a ram. Some of the witches of Thessaly were reputed to have similar powers.

'All the filth of the east drains into the Tiber', complained a Latin author in reference to the alien cultists, including Hecate worshippers, who were to be found in Rome.

The rites practised by such Asian, Egyptian and Greek sorcerers and devotees of eccentric religions were alleged by traditionalist Romans to be bloody and perverted as well as barbaric. It was said that the cultists, both foreigners and Roman citizens who had been initiated into the dark mysteries of the East, practised black magic, cannibalism, human sacrifice and sodomy. All these accusations were in time also to be made against those alleged to have attended the Witches' Sabbath.

The celebration of alien religio-magical festivals first attracted the hostile attention of the Roman authorities as early as 186 BC when 'the affair of the Bacchanalia' came to light. Originally, the Roman Bacchanalia seems to have been a fairly innocent celebration, in honour of the wine god Bacchus, which was held in daylight by an association of women. By 200 BC, however, Bacchus had become identified with the Greek god Dionysus (who was named 'the tearer of men' and reputed to confer a divine madness upon his worshippers) and the Roman Bacchanalia, now celebrated in the secrecy of night, seems to have been transformed into something very like a gathering of frenzied, perverted, and murderous witches.

Perverted worship

According to the historian Livy, men and women were initiated into the cult of the Bacchanalia by strange rituals, half religious and half magical, in the course of which huge quantities of wine were consumed. When wine had inflamed the thoughts of the initiates, said Livy, male 'mingled' with female, age with youth and all varieties of corruption began to be practised, for 'each one had at hand the pleasure to which he was most inclined'. Livy went on to assert that: 'If any of them were reluctant to submit to [sexual] abuse or to commit crime they were sacrificed . . . . To consider nothing immoral was looked upon by them as the supreme religious devotion.'

The Bacchanalia was brutally suppressed, with hundreds, perhaps thousands, of the initiates of the cult executed in every province of Italy. But other cults were imported into Rome and against them were made very similar accusations of murder, impiety, sexual perversion and cannibalism. In some cases such allegations

Classical accounts of the orgiastic revels of the worshippers of Dionysus, a god associated with the virile goat, probably contributed to the late medieval belief that witches worshipped a goat at their Sabbaths.

were, in part at least, well-founded. There is no doubt that many of the self-mutilated eunuch priests of the strange Asiatic cult of the goddess Cybele actively encouraged worshippers of the goddess to engage in buggery and masochistic scourging.

Pagan slanders

On the other hand there seems to have been no justification at all for the generally held belief of educated pagan Romans that some Christian groups of the early centuries AD engaged in practices that excelled in vileness anything associated with the Bacchanalia.

The churches of the Christians, said their opponents,

were filled with the aroma of blood. Adherents of the new faith consecrated and adored the head of a monstrous donkey, worshipped the genitals of the priests who celebrated the eucharistic rite, sacrificed babies and drank their blood, and, worst of all, practised incest – mother with son, brother with sister – as a religious rite.

In time the Church grew and, in the fourth century, became the official religion of the Roman Empire. No one any longer believed that orthodox Christians were licentious cannibals. But some Christians remembered the slanders and in time applied them to others: to pagans, heretics and, above all, witches and other supposed devil worshippers.

The cult of Dionysus, depicted here revelling with a satyr, spread from Greece to Rome at an early date. Drunken sexual orgies associated with the cult led to its suppression.

According to legend the sinful Emperor Gallicanus became a devout Christian after St Zeno, renowned for his powers of exorcism, and healed the Emperor's demon-possessed daughter.

In his first letter to the Corinthians, St Paul identified the pagan gods of Greece and Rome with the devils who served Satan. Of the animals sacrificed by pagans, he wrote, 'they are sacrificed to demons and not to God, and I would not ye should have communion with devils; ye cannot drink the cup of the Lord and the cup of demons'.

Satan's Kingdom

It seemed apparent to the early Christians that St Paul's words were the literal truth. Not just dark Hecate and flesh eating Dionysus, but Jupiter, Mercury and the bright gods of Olympus were princes of Satan's kingdom. It was they who inspired persecutions of the Church, it was they who possessed the bodies of men and women and led them into wickedness and insanity. Their machinations could, however, be defeated by the intervention of saintly Christians; a 5th-century life of St Martin of Tours records that at the sight of him those possessed by devils 'howled and trembled as criminals do when the judge arrives'. St Martin is also reported to have compelled such demons to admit their identity with the gods of Rome. 'One demoniac', recorded the saint's biographer, 'would say he was Jupiter, another

would say he was Mercury'.

It was not only pagans who were looked upon as devil worshippers. The God worshipped by unorthodox Christians, such as those many sects collectively referred to as the Gnostics, 'those who know', was in reality Satan himself. It was he who inspired the allegedly monstrous doings of these false Christians, such as human sacrifice and incest: in other words, precisely the same iniquities of which the orthodox Christians once had been accused.

Tearers of flesh

The particular servants of the demons were believed to be the *striges* – human servants of Satan with powers very similar to those attributed to witches in the later Middle Ages. One Latin grammarian defined *striges* as 'the name given to women who practise sorcery and also fly through the air'.

The *striges* did not fly on broomsticks but instead transformed themselves into birds of prey of repellent appearance and even fouler habits. They had hooked beaks capable of tearing human flesh, grasping talons, huge distorted heads and, strangely, the breasts of women. These latter, heavy with poisonous milk, they

Saint Michael, the archangel who commands the warriors of heaven in their eternal struggle against the legions of hell, was seen as the patron saint of exorcists and witch hunters.

offered to babies left lying unprotected in their cradles. Sometimes they flew to the bed of a sleeping man, returned to human shape, and had sexual intercourse with him, simultaneously draining the victim of both blood and energy.

It is apparent that the *striges* were held responsible for a good many happenings which would now be attributed to more mundane factors. Thus, what are now referred to as cot deaths, i.e., the sudden demise of young children in their sleep without obvious cause, would have been attributed to the poisonous milk of the *striges*. Similarly, male impotence resulting from physical or psychological factors was seen as the result of the activities of the *striges*. One Latin author stated that men who found their sexual powers on the wane commonly blamed the nocturnal visits of *striges* for their condition and took a curious ham and bean stew as a restorative.

Heresy and sorcery were thought of as devil-induced and, slightly paradoxically, priests and bishops were thought particularly to be subject to demonic temptings towards both.

The *striges* were often identified with both screech owls, which seem always to have had a baneful reputation in the classical world, and the *lamias* of Greek folklore, alluring but deadly females who sucked the blood of men and consumed the entrails of children.

It was probably for this reason that as late as the 16th century a common English term for a man who was wasting away as the result, so it was believed, of witchcraft, was referred to as 'owl blasted'.

It was not only the citizens of the Roman Empire who went in terror of nightriding, sexually insatiable sorceresses, who sapped men's virility and stole the life from children. For very similar beliefs seem to have been current amongst the Germanic peoples of central Europe at a very early stage, long before they had come into close contact with Latin literature and civilization. Thus, the Germanic legal code known as the Salic Laws (which dates from the 6th century, but is held by scholars to reflect the beliefs, manners and customs of an earlier age) refers to witches as holding secret meetings around a cauldron, flying through the air, and devouring the entrails of men. The name given to such a witch, *striga*, was clearly derived from late Latin, and its use provides evidence that those who compiled the Salic Code were well aware of the similarities between their own folk beliefs and those of the Roman populace.

Eaters of evil

It would seem that amongst the pagan Germans those suspected of being cannibalistic witches were themselves in some danger of being eaten, presumably as a way of destroying their evil powers. A law promulgated to the Saxons in the 8th century ordered that: 'If anyone . . . shall believe . . . that a man or woman is a *striga* and eats men, and shall on that account burn that person to death or eat his or her flesh, or give it to others to eat, he shall be executed'.

It is apparent that a belief that witches fly through the air, walk through walls and locked doors and eat men was sufficiently firmly held by the German peasantry for some women to feel sure that they themselves possessed these powers. The *Medicus*, a work compiled at the beginning of the 11th century by Burchard, Bishop of Worms, instructed priests to ask women penitents:

Have you believed . . . that in the silence of the night . . . when your husband lies in your bosom, you are able, while still in your body, to go through the closed doors and travel through the spaces of the world, together with others . . . and that without visible weapons, you kill people . . . and together cook and devour their flesh, and that where the heart was, you put straw . . . and that after eating these people you bring them alive again and grant them a brief spell of life? If you have believed this, you shall do penance on bread and water for fifty days . . . and likewise for seven years following.

Odin, who was the Scandinavian version of the Germanic Wotan, king of the gods, was believed to struggle constantly against giants, nightriders and other creatures of darkness.

The blue cloaked Odin/Wotan was invariably accompanied by the Ravens of Death and all places of execution were sacred to him — as such they were often chosen as the sites of Teutonic magical rites.

Satanic delusions

It is clear that Burchard did not believe that witches had the power of flight. Such a belief, he considered, was a satanic delusion, intended to lead men and women into thinking that there was a divine power other than God. The Bishop, however, did not doubt the reality of witchcraft of the sort known as *maleficium*, i.e., the ability to wish ill to animals and men, causing disease, death, and sexual impotence. The latter was almost always attributed to *maleficium* and was most commonly blamed on discarded mistresses or jealous wives. Accusations of sexual *maleficium* were common at every level of society and in the 9th century the Church refused, on gounds of *maleficium*, to annul the marriage of Lothair, the first king of Lorraine, to his queen in spite of the fact that it never seems to have been fully consummated. It was thought that the bewitchments of Waldrada, Lothair's mistress, had filled the king with loathing for his wife and made him incapable of achieving erection and ejaculation with anyone save Waldrada.

Waldrada was also believed to have used her enchantments to inflame Lothair with a burning desire for her sexual favours and, thus, was held to have the power of inducing both impotence and its opposite, satyriasis. Similar powers over human sexuality and its functionings are claimed at the present day by many devotees of the modern witch cult which flourishes in Britain and North America.

On the left is the great Palace of the Valhalla of Teutonic and Scandinavian myth, and on the right the world serpent whose convoluted body was explored by the northern nightriders.

By the 11th century Diana, the classical lunar goddess of whom the witch queen, Hecate, was an aspect, had become identified with Holda, a Germanic fertility deity.

Diana, the classical moon goddess, is still worshipped by some present day cultists, who claim to be the inheritors of a very ancient tradition of white, beneficent witchcraft, i.e., magic aimed at healing, not harming, those who are subjected to its influence. Whether or not such claims are wholly or partially justified is a matter of controversy.

There is no doubt, however, that the worship of Diana, who is the personification of the positive aspects of supposed lunar forces, much as Hecate personifies the negative elements of those forces, survived until long after Christianity's triumph over classical paganism. Thus, St Kilian, a Celtic missionary to the pagan Franks, was murdered when he endeavoured to persuade the peasantry to abandon their worship of Diana, and a life of St Caesarius casually mentions 'a demon whom simple folk call Diana'.

Burchard, the 11th-century writer whose opinions on the subject of nightriding cannibal witches are described on the preceding pages, gave considerable attention to Diana, whom he identified with both Herodias, the Jewish queen responsible for the death of St John the Baptist, and Holda, who seems to have been originally a Germanic fertility goddess.

The spaces of the world

In relation to Diana and her worshippers, Burchard quoted with approval a Church document which probably dated from some 200 years or so earlier. From this it is apparent that Diana was believed to lead nightriders who, while they had very similar powers of 'travelling through the spaces of the world', were far less malign than the entrail-sucking black witches of Germanic folklore. There are, affirms this document, some who: '. . . avow that in the hours of the night they ride . . . together with Diana the goddess of the pagans . . . and on particular nights are summoned to her service . . .'.

Burchard, as was said above, believed Diana to be the

same entity as Herodias – still worshipped at the present day by some self-styled white witches under the slightly altered name of Aradia – and the goddess Holda. Quite how Herodias, the somewhat obscure wife of Herod, had come to be believed to be a moon goddess endowed with awesome supernatural powers is uncertain. It may be, however, that because of her part in the execution of John the Baptist she had come to be regarded as an important female demon, who had taken on human form, which is how Diana was looked upon by the orthodox. Such an interpretation would be supported by a number of medieval sources which assert that the spirit of Herodias was sentenced to wander eternally the upper regions of the air as a punishment for her sin but, nevertheless, is allowed by God to rest herself in trees from midnight to dawn.

Souls of the dead

The identification with Holda is more apparent. In

In one of her manifestations Diana, whom the Greeks called Artemis, was a many-breasted symbolization of fertility. This was one reason for her identification with Holda.

Diana was identified also with Queen Herodias, responsible for the death of John the Baptist. The name Herodias was corrupted into Aradia, and worshipped by Italian witches, according to C.G. Leland.

Germanic folklore she and her followers, the souls of the dead, rode the winds, rewarding peasants who cultivated their lands properly, and punishing those who neglected to do so. Normally, she was a stately and beautiful mother, but when she was angry she manifested herself as a furious old hag, with long hooked nose and long and biting yellow fangs, i.e., very much the stereotype of the witch as portrayed in illustrated children's stories.

In most studies of witchcraft Diana's wild, night-riding followers are presented as being identical with the evil creatures who take the lives of both adults and children. There seems little doubt, however, that originally two quite different sets of folk beliefs were in existence. Diana and her train punished the lazy and wicked, but essentially they were benign. If, for example, they visited a peasant's home and found food and drink laid out for them they would consume it – although, magically, leaving as much as they had found – and reward the giver with a good harvest. Clearly, there were bright as well as dark aspects of popular witch beliefs.

INQUISITORS, DEMONS AND HERETICS

On 30 July 1233 Conrad of Marburg, a German inquisitor who was pious, learned, and a sadistic fanatic, was murdered on the road from Mainz. His killers were probably vassals of Henry of Seym, a nobleman whom Conrad had falsely accused of taking part in satanic orgies at which he had been seen riding a demon who had taken on the form of a gigantic crab.

Conrad's death brought an end to a persecution of supposed devil worshippers, 'Luciferians', which had terrorized the population of the huge archdiocese of Mainz and, in the course of which, large numbers of perfectly innocent people of every age and class had been burned at the stake.

The Spanish Inquisitor, which carried on its activities until some years after the French Revolution, was the last bastion of medieval beliefs concerning the appropriate punishment for magicians.

In the 16th century Catholic priests, like their predecessors of the Middle Ages, saw themselves as engaged in a battle against heresy, sorcery and the wiles of Satan.

Conrad had been in search of heretics, i.e., unorthodox Christians who had rejected the papacy and the worldliness of the Church, whom he regarded as being servants of the prince of darkness. The beliefs about the teachings and activities of heretical Christians which inspired Conrad's murderous activities were a magnified and more detailed version of the stories that had been told by pagans about the iniquitous doings of the Christians.

White as leprosy

Initiation into an heretical sect, it was said, almost always took place at night and it commenced by a demon materializing into the shape of a toad 'as big as a stove' which the candidate had to kiss on the mouth or, more usually, the anus. Next, a more important demon manifested itself, taking the form of an emaciated man, with skin 'white as leprosy' and burning coal black eyes.

Various other diabolical manifestations were succeeded by the stereotyped sexual orgy, usually involving incest and sodomy, at the conclusion of which Lucifer appeared in half human form – the upper part of his body was that of a man but 'radiant like the sun', the lower was that of an enormous tomcat. Then he was presented with a piece of the candidate's clothing, and with the acceptance of this the initiation was over.

In the very year of Conrad's death, Pope Gregory IX issued a summary of what he said were the beliefs of the heretics. They held, said the Pope, that Lucifer was the real creator of heaven and earth and would one day overthrow God and reign in glory. To please Lucifer they must do the exact opposite of what God wished them to do, and, as a reward, Lucifer would allow them subsidiary rule in his coming kingdom.

Toad worship

In reality most of those burned by Conrad were pious Catholics who had confessed to toad worship, incest and other mortal sins in order to bring to a halt the tortures to which they were submitted. Others were undoubtedly genuine heretics, men and women who were opposed to the Church and its teachings. But they were far from being Luciferians, worshippers of Satan and enemies of Christ. On the contrary, they seem to have been Waldensians, gentle and pious advocates of a pacific Christianity based on the Sermon on the Mount which had a strong resemblance to the religion of George Fox and other 17th-century Quakers.

Over the centuries which succeeded Conrad's death, accusations of the type which had been made by him were levelled at a very large number of people. Some of these were heretics whose teachings, while at odds with those of the Church, were in no way satanic. Others were perfectly orthodox Christians who had been accused of heresy because it was to someone's financial advantage to make such an accusation. There is, for example, a case on record of a young girl who had her entire family burned as heretics so that she could inherit their property and marry whom she chose.

In spite of their stereotyped pattern, accounts of Lucifer worshipping heretical practices found a ready acceptance. The same stereotypes were to recur in the great witch persecutions of the 16th and 17th centuries.

In all its essentials the 'Act of Faith' of 16th and 17th-century Spain – the burning alive of sorcerers, witches and relapsed heretics – was a repetition of the activities of medieval inquisitors.

The discovery of the physical components of a 'sorcerer's device' at a crossroads as depicted in a 14th-century manuscript. The supposed sorcerer may have been either a witch or a ritual magician.

Present day practitioners of occult techniques involving the use of ritual usually define magic by some such phrase as 'the art of causing change at will', or, in the case of those occultists who have been influenced by modern schools of depth psychology, 'the use of ritual as a means of achieving altered states of consciousness'.

Magicians of the past, however, usually took a far narrower view of the scope of ceremonial magic. As far as they were concerned the essence of the art was calling up spirits – good or bad, devils or angels – and, after entering into communication with them, persuading or binding them to carry out the magician's will.

The ritual magic of the Middle Ages had its origin in the occult techniques of spirit control which are described in surviving Graeco-Egyptian manuscripts dating from the years 100 BC to AD 400. From these, it is apparent that even at this early date the basic pattern of the rites used by magicians of the Middle Ages and the Renaissance had already been established.

Demonic magic

In essence, what the ritual magician did, or thought he did, was the same in the England of Oliver Cromwell or the Germany of the Emperor Charles v as it had been in the Alexandria of Cleopatra. He – very rarely she until modern times – began by purifying himself and his

Goya depicted these hags as both witches – servants and dupes of Satan – and as magicians, as is indicated by the *grimoire* or magical text being read aloud by one of them.

'place of working' by such means as washing himself in herbal infusions and burning astringent herbs and perfumes. Then, he would protect himself against possible demonic attack by such means as drawing a magic circle around himself or placing talismans (consecrated discs, usually made of metal, dedicated to gods or angels) in strategic positions. This magical ceremony often involved the burning of incense or the sacrifice of some animal, but its central core was the rhythmic chanting of what have been called 'the barbarous words of evocation', i.e., traditional formulae which supposedly compelled supernatural entities, whether gods, angels, or demons, to visible appearance and obedience to the magician's wishes.

Finally, supposing the spirit had been successfully evoked, the magician uttered the banishing formula which would send it back from whence it came. Failure to do this properly was considered very dangerous; numerous manuscripts and early printed books tell of magicians who were 'torn in pieces by demons' because they had foolishly neglected to utter the appropriate formula.

Those present are witches, but the protective circle delineated on the floor and the 'book of black ritual' which lies beside it indicate that they are also ceremonial magicians.

In Anglo-Saxon times magicians were thought to have close relations with demons – but, unlike the witches of late medieval belief, they were reputed to be the masters, not the servants, of devils.

Hell broth

The employment of magic of this sort was an element of many witchcraft trials of the 16th and 17th centuries. The witchcraft, in which the inquisitors and other persecutors of witches believed, was not merely the 'pure' witchcraft of the anthropologist, no more than the supposed use of a malignant inner force with which some people were endowed. It was a blend of a number of techniques and processes, real or imaginary, which were understood as forming a coherent body of theory and practice.

Firstly, there was the supposed ability of some to wish ill to others, of which the 'evil eye' was the most obvious example. Secondly, there was sorcery, i.e., the manipulation of physical matter for occult purposes as was, and is, done by practitioners of image magic. Thirdly, there was ritual magic, involving relationships with discarnate spirits. And, finally, there was the myth of the Witches' Sabbath, which had its origins both in stories of perverted orgies, engaged in by groups as disparate as devotees of Hecate and Dionysus, early Christians and medieval heretics, and the demonology of St Thomas Aquinas and the scholastic philosophers of the Middle Ages.

29

Those who were accused of witchcraft during the great persecutions of the period 1450–1700 were believed to be guilty of an enormous variety of crimes against the laws of God and man – of the malicious destruction of their neighbours' crops and animals; of murder, usually by ill wishing, the evil eye, or the employment of image magic, but sometimes by human sacrifice; of cannibalism, rape, sodomy and incest.

In the view of those who conducted the persecutions such crimes were detestable but, in a sense, minor. The greatest offence of which anyone could be capable was, or so it was thought, the offering of worship in its fullest form to anyone save God. Witches were believed to offer such worship to Lucifer, lightbearer of darkness, eternal adversary of good, and those fallen angels who were his servitors in the courts of hell. This was the black sin of witches, their monstrous offence against the divine order which merited death in this world and damnation in the next.

Demonology and magic

In the final analysis, such an attitude derived from concepts which were developed in their most sophisticated forms by Christian philosophers and theologians of the Middle Ages. It would not be going too far to say that the logical and rigidly ordered way in which the scholastic philosophers of the Middle Ages applied their reasoning powers to the subjects of demonology and ritual magic shaped the beliefs and guided the

By the 16th century scholastic teachings concerning magic and witchcraft had resulted in an anachronistic belief that the first Christians were concerned with witchcraft in much the same way as inquisitors of the Renaissance period.

It was believed by the scholastics that the central core of ritual magic was the offering of *latria* to beings who were God's creations. As such, it necessarily involved sin; whether the spirits called upon by magicians were supposedly evil, morally neutral or even good was quite unimportant. By the very act of evoking them magicians were engaging in the unlawful bestowal of *latria* and, by doing so, were condemning their own souls.

Illusion

In fact, of course, St Thomas Aquinas and the scholastics did not believe that the spirits with which ritual magicians held communion were ever good or even neutral. Demons were believed to be everywhere and to be capable of appearing in an infinity of illusory forms. They could, for example, take the forms of insects in order to distract holy men from their devotions, of angels and good spirits in order to delude magicians and lead them to destruction, and of harmless looking domestic animals. If an account given by Richalmus, a 13th-century abbot, is to be believed, they could even produce indigestion. According to Richalmus, he had actually heard two demons considering how they could prevent him from saying Mass: 'One demon asked the other to make me hoarse, the other said he would instead give me an attack of flatulence'.

Comic enough, perhaps. But equally ludicrous stories and the beliefs from which they derived were to send thousands to the stake.

The beliefs of St Thomas Aquinas, greatest of the scholastic philosophers of the Middle Ages, concerning demons and their relationships with humanity, exerted an abiding influence on inquisitors and witch hunters.

actions of those who persecuted witches in succeeding centuries.

The scholastics, so called because they taught in Paris, Oxford and the other great theological schools of Europe, differentiated between two sorts of worship, *latria* and *dulia*. The latter was defined as meaning something like 'proper respect' or 'reverence', and it was considered that this sort of worship was due from an inferior to a superior, e.g., from an ordinary Christian to a saint. *Latria*, however, was regarded as the worship which was properly owed to God only, but could be sinfully given to other creatures. St Thomas Aquinas, perhaps the greatest and certainly the most influential of the scholastics, considered that the most grievous of sins was the wrongful bestowal of *latria*. He wrote:

> . . . *just as the worst crime in an earthly kingdom would be for a man to give royal honour to other than the true king . . . so in sins against God . . . the greatest is for man to give divine honour to a creature . . . since he thus sets up another God in the world and lessens the divine sovereignty.*

St Thomas Aquinas sees the lips of the image of the crucified Christ move and hears them utter the words 'Well hast thou written of me Thomas'.

THE DEVIL'S FAITH

By the middle of the 15th century, belief in an organized satanic conspiracy, the witch cult, had become well established.

Peasant folk's beliefs about sinister nightriders, Catholic misunderstandings of the nature of the worship engaged in by medieval heretics, a knowledge of the magical techniques used by village 'cunning men' and 'wise women' had all become combined with the demonological speculations of theologians.

The resulting hell-broth was a belief in the existence of witchcraft as a 'Church of Satan' with its own hierarchy and festivals.

The witches of ancient Greece were popularly believed to steal the noses from both corpses and living men whom they had thrown into a trance. Those of 15th-century Germany were reputed to behave even more alarmingly: they would painlessly remove the genital organs of sleeping men, and carry them off and hide them in monstrous nests situated in high trees.

One German village, reports a 15th-century account, was so afflicted by such pestiferous activity that the peasants instituted a search for the nest which contained the local witches' curious collection. Eventually, to the joy of all, it was discovered and found to include the penis of the village priest, which was immediately recognized 'because it was so much larger than any of the others'.

The extraordinary thing about this mildly improper story is not that it was written – anticlerical jokes have been around for a very long time – but that it was seriously recounted as truth in a treatise on witchcraft written by two learned Dominican friars.

A witch hunter's textbook

The treatise in question was *Malleus Maleficarum*, a punning Latin title meaning 'the hammer of the witches', which was first printed in 1486. It quickly became looked upon as the most authoritative study of witchcraft and methods of detecting it, and it was frequently reprinted.

The authors of this textbook, Jakob Sprenger and Heinrich Kramer, had been inquisitors in the Austrian Tyrol where there had been many complaints about their brutality towards those whom they had interrogated, and it seems virtually certain that they produced *Malleus Maleficarum* as a defence of their activities. Their intention seems to have been to show that the witch cult was so vile that it was justifiable to use all methods, including torture, in carrying out investigations into the beliefs of those suspected of adherence to the cult. They also, it is apparent, wished to counter scepticism concerning the more amazing claims made by the Church in regard to the supernatural powers of witches.

The evil eye

Some people, said Kramer and Sprenger, wrongly believe that witchcraft and demons exist only in 'the imagination of the ignorant and vulgar' who attribute 'the natural accidents which happen to a man . . . to

The genius of Goya enabled him to express a synthesis of classical beliefs concerning Pan with elements derived from the writing of the inquisitors of the 15th and 16th centuries.

some supposed devil'. This, they said, was in clear contradiction to the doctrines of the Church 'which teaches us that certain angels fell and . . . can do many wonderful things . . .'. These wonderful things included not only inflicting disease and causing storms and tempests, but also moving witches, houses and even whole fields through the air from one place to another. The very fact that such things were humanly impossible, wrote the ingenious inquisitors, proved that demons were at work upon the earth.

Witches, the servants of Satan and his attendant demons, could even use the powers their masters had given them against the judges who tried them. They can, says the *Malleus* 'bewitch their judges by a mere glance from their eyes'. The *Malleus* is a sinister book and its evil influence led to many deaths. Perhaps the worst thing about it was the approval it gave to torture as a means of inducing confession. The attitude of Kramer and Sprenger towards this is illustrated by their reference to two witches who were 'questioned gently . . . being suspended by their thumbs'.

Malleus Maleficarum and other printed treatises on the subjects of witchcraft and demonology gave much attention to the festivals believed to be celebrated by large groups of witches. From the evidence given at witch trials and from the statements of self-confessed initiates of the witch cult a certain pattern can be discerned in the dates on which festivals had allegedly taken place.

Virgin Mary, the day on which the Virgin underwent ritual purification in the Temple of Jerusalem and, so tradition avers, lit a candle to signify that her son would be 'the light of the world'. But long before Christianity reached western Europe the beginning of February was marked by a fire festival, the purpose of which was to induce the goddess of spring to drive away darkness and bring warmth to the soil.

An old witch anoints her younger sister with the strange unguents which empowered her transportation to the annual feast of hell held in the wilds of the Black Mountains.

It would seem that each year there were six great festivals of the cult. These were Candlemas, 2 February; May Eve, 30 April; St John's Eve, 23 June; Lammastide, 1 August; Hallowe'en, 31 October; and St Thomas's Day, 21 December.

If groups of anti-Christian, or, at any rate, pagan cultists really did celebrate religious festivals on those dates, it seems likely that organized witchcraft was not a mere fantasy of Sprenger, Kramer and other inquisitors but was a survival of a very old fertility religion. For the six dates all have a certain relationship to very ancient pagan beliefs in spite of the fact that some of them are also significant in the calendar of the Church.

A base stinking idol

Candlemas is the feast of the Purification of the Blessed

May Eve and the following day also had a Christian significance, being dedicated to Walburga, an English saint who died in 8th-century Germany. But it was also the greatest of the festivals of pagan Europe, a celebration of the fertility of crops, animals and human beings. One 17th-century Calvinist referred to the Maypole as a 'base stinking idol' and he and his coreligionists seem to have been well aware that this seemingly innocent symbol of rustic jollity originally had a phallic significance.

Similarly, St John's Eve coincided with the old pagan midsummer festival, St Thomas's Day, with the midwinter feast Hallowe'en, the eve of the day dedicated to all Christian saints, with the pagan festival of the dead, and Lammastide was originally the old pagan festival of harvest home. The word 'Lammas' is a corruption of 'Loaf Mass': the Church had endeavoured to put a

Christian veneer on old heathen wood by instituting a Mass in honour of the loaf made from the first reapings of the ripened grain.

The old religion?

If it could be proved that organized societies of witches existed in the Middle Ages and succeeding centuries, and if it could be shown that they did, indeed, hold celebratory rites on the dates of ancient pagan festivals, it would be very strong evidence that, as the late Dr Margaret Murray and others have contended, an old religion of fertility survived into modern times and was named witchcraft by its Christian enemies.

The evidence presented in favour of such a survival is, however, extremely suspect, much of it being derived from confessions extracted under torture or threat of torture. What could be more likely than that witchcraft suspects would admit to taking part in old pagan festivals, because it was made clear to them that they would only prolong the agonies inflicted on them unless they made such admissions? In any case such confessions contain such fantastic statements about the nature of the supposed festivals, 'Witches' Sabbaths', that it would be unwise to give them any credence whatsoever. One can only compare them with the 'voluntary confessions' made to the Gestapo.

A human sacrifice to Satan, here portrayed by Goya under the conventional appearance of a horned goat, was believed to be the high point of the great festivals of the witches' calendar.

Witches supposedly departed via the chimney – much wider than its modern equivalent – when they set off for the weird rites that were held to celebrate the major Satanic 'holy days'.

During a 16th-century siege of Calais two soldiers on guard duty noticed a small and jet black cloud drifting low in an otherwise clear sky. From it there came sounds resembling those made by a crowd of people engaged in animated conversation. After some conversation one of the soldiers aimed his arquebus, a 16th-century musket, at the cloud and fired.

At their feet, wounded in the thigh, fell a very fat, very drunken naked woman who, when asked to explain herself and her ability to fly 'pretended to be half witted'. So said the author of a treatise on demonology, who said he had been present at the siege and spoken to the soldier whose markmanship had produced such a disconcerting result.

It is a reasonable conjecture that what really happened, if anything happened at all, was that the soldier fired upwards and that his bullet, dropping back to earth, had hit a naked harlot plying her trade behind a nearby bush. But the demonologist who wrote of the matter was quite sure that the woman was a witch journeying to or, more probably in view of her drunkenness, from the Witches' Sabbath.

The feast of the goat

The Witches' Sabbath, sometimes referred to as 'the synagogue of Satan', was believed to be a combination of a sexually perverted cannibalistic orgy with blasphemous Satan worship. This latter was supposedly the physical adoration of, and submission to, the Devil in a quite literal sense. It was believed that Lucifer, most commonly in the form of a black goat, materialized at the Sabbath, presided over the hellish revelries, and copulated with all or some of the women present.

Descriptions of what happened at the Sabbath show considerable variations in witchcraft confessions between one country and another. Thus, for example, German and Basque witches confessed to cannibalism

Peasant witches gather at the Sabbath for drunken feasting, bizarre sexuality, and the darker pleasures of human sacrifice and payment of homage to the lords of hell.

Old witches instruct a young neophyte in the techniques of journeying to the Sabbath, where she will be initiated into even darker mysteries.

sometimes took the form of a man but more commonly appeared in 'some horrid shape, either a goat or dog'. One by one the witches made some form of obeisance to their master; usually this homage took the form of the *osculum obscenum*, kissing the Devil's anus.

The main features of the Sabbath were always a feast followed by a sexual orgy. Neither would seem to have been particularly attractive if some confessions are to be believed. Frequently the food was vile in appearance, smell and taste, while the wine resembled 'black clotted blood'. Sexual couplings were sometimes equally unappealing. Satan had connection with all the women present, but his genitals were hard and scaly, his seed 'cold as ice', and his embraces painful in the extreme.

If the Witches' Sabbath ever took place at all, it is apparent that those who participated in it had masochistic tastes.

The participants in this Sabbatic gathering seem to be of a higher social standing than that of most of those accused of witchcraft. Nevertheless, like their peasant sisters, they were looked upon as Lucifer's accomplices.

more frequently than English witches. Nevertheless, a fairly clear pattern of Sabbath ritual and revel can be discerned from the confessions made by those tried for witchcraft in countries as distant from one another as Sweden and Spain. This sometimes has been thought to indicate that such confessions, however fantastic, indicated an underlying reality, the survival in Christian Europe of an ancient fertility religion to which many of the peasantry still adhered. It has to be remembered, however, that almost all those who confessed to attendance at the Sabbath did so under torture, and one can safely assume that they confessed whatever their torturers expected them to confess.

Wine like clotted blood

The Sabbath began with the lighting of what the demonologist Guazzo called a 'foul and horrid fire' from which the assembled witches lit torches or black candles. By their flickering light the unholy congregation witnessed the appearance of their god, who

WITCH WORSHIP

Goya, a non-believer in the existence of witchcraft, regarded what he thought of as the myth of witch worship as an expression of the evil which lurks in the mind of every human being.

Satan worship took many forms, from the simple homage of the *osculum obscenum* – in the words of one arraignment 'the kissing with sacrilegious mouth the Devil's most foul and beastly posterior' – to elaborate parodies of the rites and ceremonies of the Church and the solemn defilement of holy things and substances.

As far as Catholics were (and are) concerned the holiest of all substances was the host, the consecrated wafer which, while retaining the outward form of bread, is in substance the Body and Blood of Christ. Therefore, it is not surprising that in Catholic countries witches were believed to take a particular delight in submitting the consecrated host to blasphemous indignities. In 1582, for example, some French witches were charged with 'keeping in your mouths the Most Holy Sacrament . . . execrably spitting it out upon the ground . . . thus worshipping, honouring and glorifying the Devil . . .'.

The way of reversal

Charges of blasphemous defilement of the host and the parodying of orthodox worship were surprisingly uncommon in the early decades of the great witch persecution of the period 1450–1700, but it became increasingly frequent in the 16th and 17th centuries. This is at least partially explained by the fact that some people, proletarian Protestants, did undoubtedly en-

gage in what Catholics regarded as coarse blasphemies in the years subsequent to the Reformation. Thus a Protestant farmer of the early 16th century was charged with heresy because he was heard to remark of the consecrated host that he himself 'threshed God Almighty out of straw', while another, on hearing a Church bell, was heard to remark that it was 'fit to hang about any cow's neck', and during the reign of Mary Tudor a London priest walking in procession behind the host had a large pudding dropped into his hands by a jeering bystander.

There is no doubt, however, that while such Protestant pleasantries account for some 16th-century accusations of blasphemy, those alleged to worship Satan were believed to have gone much further, even to have engaged in what is called 'the way of reversal'.

Infernal atavism

Atavism is a return to the source, a moving back through time, or a retracing of a journey through time, so that an earlier stage of existence is re-experienced. The witches' way of reversal was the deliberate inversion of all normal modes of behaviour, the taking of a path the nature of which is summed up in the phrase 'evil be thou my good'. It has been suggested by some modern occultists that the witches' way of reversal was an 'infernal atavism', an esoteric pathway which, it was

The Devil was believed to baptize newly-initiated members of the witch cult by sprinkling them with an infernal liquid of which the main ingredient was 'sticking urine'.

The posterior kiss has always been interpreted as a symbol of the most abject submission. Those accused of conferring it on the Devil have included pagans, heretics and witches.

thought, would lead eventually to time flowing backwards, and Lucifer regaining his place in heaven.

This sounds extremely far fetched. Nevertheless, it has to be admitted that a total reversal of every normal mode of behaviour was a consistent feature of witch worship – if one believes in the truth of witchcraft confessions.

Thus, the presiding officer at the Sabbath sprinkled his congregation with a 'Holy Water', i.e., stinking urine; he conducted a rite at which he distributed loathsome sacraments of black bread, 'tasting like dung', and foul water. This reversal of religious custom was, said the demonologist Guazzo, reflected in the way in which witches 'moved' their bodies in the course of their worship. They walked like crabs or with their faces turned to the sky, 'they do all things in a manner foreign to the use of other men'. It seems likely that Guazzo and those who wrote in similar vein were expressing their own masochistic fantasies and desires rather than making statements of fact.

Trampling on the 'cross' – a symbolic rejection of Christ, his Church and its teachings – was believed by inquisitors to be an integral part of the worship of Lucifer.

THE WITCHES' PHARMACY

The forked mandrake root, in appearance vaguely resembling the legs and genitals of a naked human being, was used extensively in the manufacture of love charms and amulets.

From classical times until the present day witches, both black and white, have been renowned for their knowledge of the healing, poisonous and magical properties of herbs. The traditional wisdom of 'cunning men', 'wise women' and 'white witches' may have been exaggerated at times. There is real doubt, however, that some peasant healers of the past employed effective herbal remedies and that their patients had a better chance of recovery than those treated by the violent purgings and bleedings which were then in vogue amongst orthodox medical practitioners.

Similarly, it seems safe to assume that at least some of those men and women who were charged with the murder of their neighbours by sorcery and black magic were, in fact, poisoners who had applied their knowledge of herbal pharmacy to evil ends.

Oil and plover's blood

There was only a thin line between the use of herbs as

poisons and their employment as remedies. Thus, for example, peasant midwives, who were frequently credited with dabbling in witchcraft of both black and white varieties, seem to have been prepared sometimes to bring the lives of deformed babies to a premature end by an administration of a poisonous decoction of foxgloves. Yet the same decoction, once known as oil of foxgloves and containing the poisonous alkaloid, digitalis, is an effective remedy for certain types of heart disease and was used for this purpose by white witches. It was, in fact, from peasant healers that orthodox physicians first acquired a knowledge of the pharmaceutical properties of digitalis, a synthetic equivalent of

Witches preparing a hell-broth, compounded of snakes, cockerels' blood and venomous plants, with the object of raising storms to destroy their neighbours' crops.

40

Witches were reputed to employ the fruits of the mandrake, renowned for its magical properties since ancient Egypt, to induce both death and sexual frenzy in their victims.

which is still the usual prescription for some varieties of cardiac disorder.

Herbs were also credited with strictly magical properties; it was even held possible to use herbs to make people who were *not* witches believe that they were. One such herb and its supposed effects was described in *The Little Book of the Secrets of Albertus Magnus*, a textbook of peasant sorcery and witchcraft which was compiled in 18th-century France:

> . . . *if it be joined with the blood of a female lapwing or black plover, and put with oil in a lamp, all that are present when it is lighted shall believe themselves to be witches, so that one shall believe of another that his head is in heaven and his feet on earth . . .*

In other words, effects similar to those produced by LSD and other psychedelic drugs were supposedly produced.

The witches' ointment

The witches of ancient Thessaly were believed to compound unguents which had powers of transforming human beings into animals and conferring the ability to fly. This was to prove an abiding traditional belief, and the use of 'flying ointments' by alleged witches featured in the evidence given at many trials and in some confessions. The victims of a Swedish trial of 1669 confessed that Satan had given them 'a horn with a salve in it with which we do anoint ourselves before flying to the Sabbath', while five years earlier some English witches had made similar admissions to the use of a raw-smelling green oil which they had rubbed into their wrists and foreheads.

Some recipes for such ointments have survived and include herbs which are known to have the property of inducing delusions. One 16th-century writer gave such a recipe as consisting of 'the fat of young children' to which had to be added 'eleoselinum, aconitum, frondes populeas and soote'. Two of these substances which in large doses can kill, but in small amounts produce hallucinations, including delusions of flying, might have been absorbed through their application to the broken skin of a louse-ridden peasant of the 16th century.

Witches may never have flown, but it is possible that some of those who experimented with witches' ointments genuinely believed that they had done so.

41

A highly stylized 19th-century witch-doll with a written curse. Clearly, this type of folk magic was being practised until a very late date.

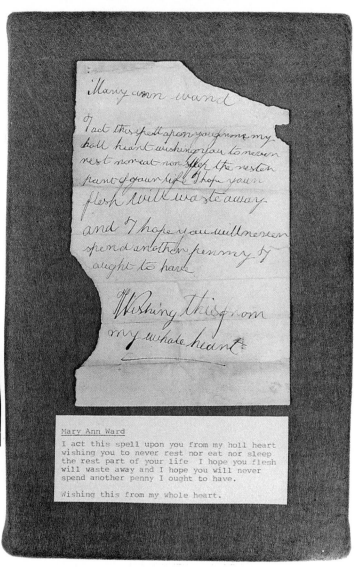

Mary Ann Ward
I act this spell upon you from my holl heart wishing you to never rest nor eat nor sleep the rest part of your life I hope you flesh will waste away and I hope you will never spend another penny I ought to have.

Wishing this from my whole heart.

Throughout history dolls have been employed for two purposes. Firstly, as children's playthings, and secondly as the instruments of the bewitchments of love and death, an integral part of the witch faith.

Those used for the latter purpose have sometimes been of sinister appearance and composition, but few can have been quite so unpleasant as the death doll which the American journalist, W.B. Seabrook, saw in the hinterlands of Liberia in the late 1920s. It was, reported Seabrook, a human corpse coated with tar in order to slow down the processes of decomposition. The monstrous doll was clad in sweat-stained clothing stolen from the sorcerer's intended victim. This last was intended to establish a magical link between 'doll' and victim, and the use of such a technique has been associated frequently with the image magic employed by witches and sorcerers. Typically, the link was created by moulding some of the victim's hair or nail clippings into the substance from which the doll was made. Use of discarded or stolen clothing, particularly that soaked in 'vital juices', i.e., sweat and other body secretions, was also considered effective.

This doll, in a model coffin, was found by firemen in a London house. From the shape of the coffin it is clear that it is of comparatively recent origin.

Thirteen needles

Whether or not witchcraft ever existed as an organized cult, holding great Sabbaths at which every variety of perversity was indulged in by the participants, there can be no doubt at all that throughout history sorcerers, wise women and devotees of ritual magic have used dolls for the purpose of bewitching others.

Dolls have been used more commonly with the intention of inflicting harm or bringing death than of inducing love. Even when utilized for the latter purpose, witcheries involving dolls have often been somewhat sinister and the concepts of sexuality and death seem to have been intertwined with one another. Thus, a formula contained in a late Egyptian text instructs the male sorcerer who wishes to command the sexual services of a woman to begin by making a wax image of the object of his desires. The image was then pierced with 13 needles in the hands, feet, ears, eyes, forehead, mouth, navel, anus and pubic area.

This sounds more like a death spell than a love spell, and the next stage of the process was even more grisly. At sunset the doll was placed upon the fresh grave of someone who had either died young or by violence. Then the terrible gods and goddesses of the underworld were invoked to give their aid in awakening from its rest the soul of the person whose remains were buried there.

Psychic rape

The sorcerer instructed the spirit of the corpse to obsess the desired woman:

> . . . Let her sleep with none other, let her have no pleasurable intercourse with any man save me alone. Let her neither eat nor drink, nor love, nor be strong or well, let her have no sleep except with me . . .

As Richard Cavendish pointed out in his study, *The Magical Arts*, this 'love spell' amounted to carrying out psychic rape with the assistance of a zombie.

Murder, not rape, has been the more usual motive of those who have experimented with doll magic, and those who have believed in its efficacy have included not only peasant devotees of folk magic but aristocratic students of ritual magic.

Typical of the first category were John Palmer and Elizabeth Knott, executed at St Albans in 1649 for killing a woman by roasting a doll upon a fire. A more aristocratic magician was John of Nottingham, who in 1324 attempted to kill King Edward II and six of his courtiers by driving 'curious pins wrought of sharp lead' into the heads of waxen dolls.

There can be no doubt that doll magic, whether or not it is efficacious, has often been used by men and women with murderous intentions.

This deathly doll, found in Norfolk in 1964, almost certainly was made at some time in the present century. Now, as for thousands of years past, doll magic is practised.

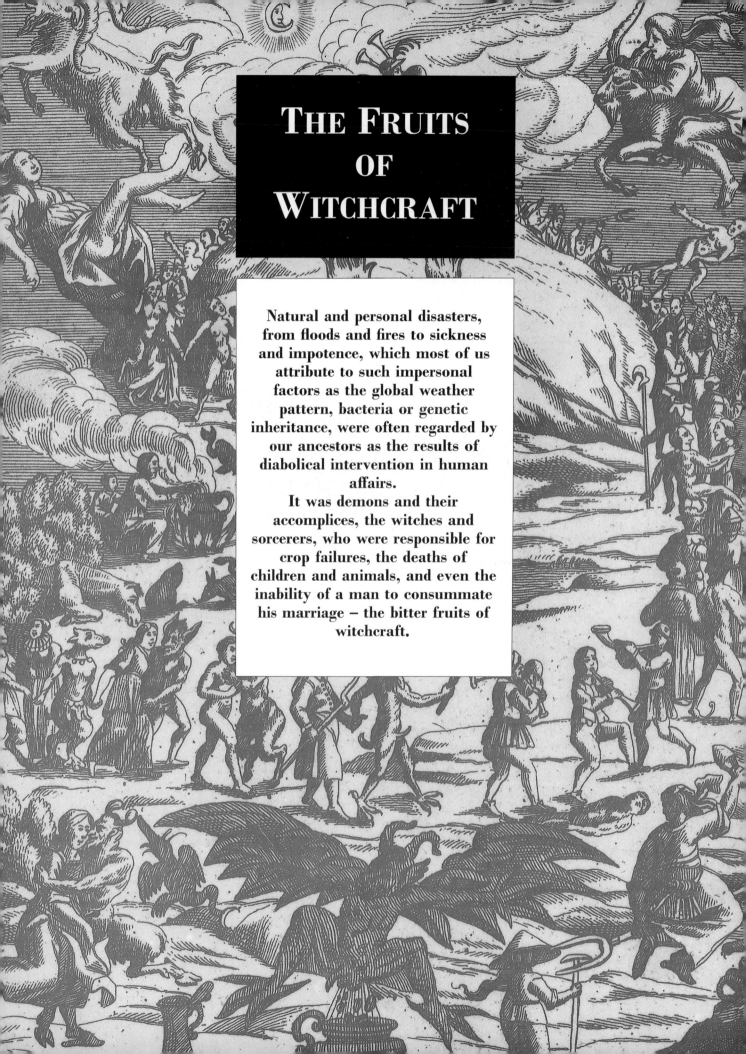

THE FRUITS
OF
WITCHCRAFT

Natural and personal disasters, from floods and fires to sickness and impotence, which most of us attribute to such impersonal factors as the global weather pattern, bacteria or genetic inheritance, were often regarded by our ancestors as the results of diabolical intervention in human affairs.

It was demons and their accomplices, the witches and sorcerers, who were responsible for crop failures, the deaths of children and animals, and even the inability of a man to consummate his marriage – the bitter fruits of witchcraft.

THE TEMPTATIONS OF VIRTUE

The Gospel story of Satan's temptation of Christ, during the latter's 40 days in the wilderness, was the prototype of a host of pious legends concerning experiences undergone by saints.

'The whole race of devils', said Saint Athanasius, 'is beyond measure . . . jealous of all mankind and particularly of the monks . . .'

If the lives of the saints and the writings of the chroniclers of the Middle Ages are to be believed, this demonic jealousy found practical outlet in determined efforts to seduce holy men and women from the paths of virtue.

Anthony, a third-century Egyptian saint, was believed to have been peculiarly virtuous by his contemporaries; that is to say he was chaste, spent a great deal of time in prayer, never washed and lived on a diet consisting mainly of mouldy bread. If the latter was infected with the fungus known as ergot, which induces hallucinations, it would explain the saint's claim to have been subjected to demonic temptations of quite exceptional severity and unpleasantness. Devils thrust themselves on the saint's vision in the forms of wolves, lions, serpents and scorpions. They also sent him 'filthy and maddening thoughts' and on one occasion induced their prince, Satan, to manifest himself under the similitude of a beautiful and lecherous woman. Even this last temptation was resisted successfully by the saint. Not all monks, however, were as successful in repelling the assaults of the Evil One.

Roasted monk

The Italian demonologist, Guazzo, reported the case of some monks who had so fallen victim to the wiles of demons, that they habitually slept with harlots.

One evening one of these fallen monks blasphemously thanked Satan, not God, for the meal he had eaten. All three found this amusing: 'they left the table with laughter and went off to the dormitory, each with his wench'. Almost immediately there entered three demons through the bolted door. They seized the blasphemous monk, spitted and roasted him so thoroughly that 'the room was full of the stench of burned flesh'.

This was no dream, wrote Guazzo, because in the morning the other monks found their brother's body 'quite blackened and burned'.

Lust and blasphemy

It is significant that it was only the blasphemous monk of Guazzo's story who was roasted and that his two companions, as lecherous as himself, escaped unharmed.

Lust was, it would seem, regarded as the least culpable of the seven deadly sins, a fact illustrated by a story told by Caesarius, a 13th-century demonologist, concerning a nun whom devils tempted with lustful desires. Her prayers for relief from the temptation to lechery were answered by the vision of an angel which instructed her to recite the verse of a psalm when tempted.

This worked excellently but now she was tempted by other demons to blaspheme. She called on the angel who suggested another verse as an antidote but told her that its use would restore all her lusts. She chose to follow this course for 'it is better for one's body to burn with desire than for one's soul to burn in hellfire'.

The 13th-century Abbot Richalmus claimed to have seen demons of the sort which afflicted the unfortunate French nun. He had observed them, so he said, surrounding monks as wholly as water a bather. But demons could, it was believed, enter a human body as well as surround it.

Invisible arrows shot by witches at their victims were thought sometimes to be the cause of many human ills, from lameness to madness and demonic possession.

Childish fantasy

Symptoms of possession seem frequently to have been the results of combinations of childish fantasies, hysteria and outright fraud, designed to substantiate the accusations made by disturbed children and adolescents.

Such fraud was proved in an English 'possession' of 1620. The victim of the demon was a schoolboy who seemed to be vomiting pins and other unlikely objects

A delineation of the sort of demon believed to be capable of entering and dominating the mind and body of an individual and using both for its own diabolic purposes.

In May 1966 six people in Switzerland became convinced that Bernadette Hasler, a 17-year-old girl, was in league with the powers of hell, thus a witch, and possessed by a demon. Following a very old course recommended by some 16th and 17th-century demonologists, they decided to conduct an exorcism which would be accompanied by heavy beatings 'to drive the devils out'.

After prolonged physical and mental tortures, the girl wrote a confession which was reminiscent of admissions of witchcraft made three centuries earlier. Satan, said Bernadette, had visited her, had had sexual intercourse with her and had promised her that one day she would be 'Queen of the World'. Bernadette died of the injuries she had suffered during the beatings and, in 1969, a Zurich court found the six exorcists guilty of her unlawful killing.

Although the Zurich case is comparatively recent, it does illustrate a point which is of historical importance. Those possessed were usually looked upon as innocent victims of demons. Sometimes, however, it was suspected that they had opened themselves voluntarily to satanic forces by either engaging in witchcraft or, as Bernadette was alleged to have done, making love to demons.

Here Goya depicts the terrors which afflict the bewitched and the possessed. Whether such terrors come from outside influences or from the forces of the unconscious mind, they are a *reality*.

and whose urine had turned a sinister blue. He also exhibited one of the classic signs of demon infestation by going into convulsions when he heard the opening words of the Gospel of St John. Or rather, when he heard them in English, for a learned man had read them to him in Greek without any untoward result. This aroused suspicion of fraud which was turned into certainty when the boy was caught inserting ink soaked paper beneath the foreskin of his penis.

The boy seems to have escaped any penalty for the antics he had indulged in, save a beating. Not all childish pretence and hysteria ended quite so uneventfully. It seems likely, for example, that a woman named Louise Maillat died in the France of the 1620s because of a silly game she had played almost 30 years earlier.

The game of murder

In the summer of 1598 Louise, then an eight-year-old girl, was afflicted either with a neurological disorder or, more probably, decided to make herself the centre of adult attention by behaving in a very peculiar manner.

She reverted from walking to crawling and 'kept twisting her mouth about'. This continued for some weeks, at the end of which her anxious parents called in an exorcist to drive out the demons which, so they thought, were afflicting her.

Under cross examination by the exorcist five demons – Cat, Dog, Griffon, Jolly and Wolf – spoke through the child's mouth and said they were controlled by a woman named Françoise Sécrétain. The childish names given by Louise to her 'demons' indicated an immature imagination, but Françoise was arrested, tortured and, after admitting to being a witch, to persecuting Louise and to having the usual sexual relationships with demons, was executed. A little girl's game had been taken seriously and she had become responsible for a death – in effect, an eight-year-old had become a murderess.

It seems likely, however, that little Louise was herself regarded with some suspicion and was kept under close watch for many years afterwards. Certainly a mature woman of the same name was executed for witchcraft almost 30 years later.

47

The Devil and his attendant demons would seem to have shown always a special interest in convents and those who inhabit them, and in 16th and 17th-century France diabolical possession and obsession became almost an occupational disease amongst nuns.

The first outbreak of what came to be a psychic epidemic was recorded at a Cambrai convent in 1491 and the symptoms exhibited by the possessed nuns followed a pattern which was to become fairly common-place. The women concerned would behave normally most of the time but, occasionally, would have what were called fits. They were clearly hysterical episodes, in which they barked like dogs, made disgusting noises,

blasphemed, performed feats of physical strength of which normally they would have been incapable, and purported to foretell the future.

It seemed clear that demons were at work and that witchcraft was involved; almost inevitably one of the nuns who had been affected was declared to be a witch, was removed elsewhere and the outbreak ceased.

Psychosexual fantasy

It is likely that the symptoms of 'possession' exhibited by the nuns of Cambrai were, in reality, symptoms of sexual repression and neuroses. Certainly, it is clear

A nun, seemingly in a rapture of contemplation, but actually under diabolic attack as depicted in the 1920s' Swedish film *Witches* (Häxan).

The outbreak of supposed demonic possession which took place in 1634 at the convent in Loudun was the subject of a book by Aldous Huxley which later was made into a Ken Russell film, *The Devils.*

6,666 Devils

As time went by Madeleine's symptoms increased in intensity. She, or the 6,666 demons who supposedly possessed her, continually babbled filth and blasphemy and talked of her sexual relations with Gaufridi and the latter's attendance at the Witches' Sabbath.

Such behaviour was infectious and several other nuns began to claim that they too were possessed. Exorcisms proved ineffectual and Gaufridi, at first protesting his innocence, was arrested, accused of witchcraft and submitted to brutal tortures which induced him to sign a confession. In this he admitted attendance at the Sabbath, eating children, initiating Madeleine into witchcraft and, by sorcery, seducing over 1,000 women.

In court Gaufridi retracted his confession, but Madeleine's behaviour in court, which included having a violent orgasm at the sight of Gaufridi and claiming to have accompanied him to the Sabbath, ensured the priest's conviction and sent him to his death.

Gaufridi's execution was followed by the cessation of Madeleine's symptoms of demonic possession, but not of her troubles. For the rest of her life she was the object of ecclesiastical suspicion – she had, after all, admitted attending the Sabbath – and in 1652 she was charged with witchcraft, found guilty and sentenced to life imprisonment. She survived until 1677.

Urbain Grandier, the priest and supposed accomplice of Satan, who was held to be guilty of inducing the possessions at Loudun and executed after monstrous torture.

that psychosexual fantasies were involved in several similar outbreaks which took place in the 17th century – at Aix in 1611, at Loudun in 1634, at Louviers in 1647 and at Auxonne in 1660. The first of these, which can be regarded as typical, resulted from the erotic hysteria of a young Ursuline nun, Madeleine de Demandoix Palud, who had been born in 1593.

As a very young girl, Madeleine had been a boarder in an Ursuline convent but had been sent back to her parents, who lived in Marseilles, suffering from home-sickness. The young Madeleine had, as her confessor, a Marseilles priest named Louis Gaufridi with whom she fell in love. It is possible that Gaufridi returned her affections. Certainly her parents suspected that this was so and Madeleine claimed that she had been seduced by the priest when she had been only 13. To get her away from Gaufridi's influence, real or imaginary, she was sent to the convent at Aix where, in 1609, she began to exhibit the symptoms of possession such as convulsions, uncontrollable outbursts of rage at the sight of holy objects, and speaking in a strange voice.

THE WITCHCRAFT OF DEATH

A small gathering of witches in a hayloft who have evoked a demon in the performance of a spell. The fanged viper indicates the spell's murderous intent.

The malice of witches was almost unbounded. Not only did the members of the cult inflict sickness and lingering death on those who caused them annoyance, often of a very petty nature, but they deliberately murdered large numbers of totally innocent people by poisoning wells and spreading the plague. So, at any rate, said the 16th and 17-century writers of treatises on witchcraft and demonology.

Just how small a personal slight a witch would take as a suitable motivation for murder is illustrated by the accusations made in 1602 against a family named Trevisard, who dwelt in the Devonshire township of Hardness.

On one occasion, said a woman named Alice Butler, her servant Alice Beere refused to lend Michael Trevisard a hatchet. 'Shall I not have it?', said Trevisard, 'I will do thee a good turn ere twelve month be at an end'. Presumably, he spoke ironically for in the words of Alice Butler's deposition:

And shortly the said Alice Beere sickened, continuing one day well and another day ill, for the space of eleven weeks, and then died . . . both the husband of this examinate [Alice Butler] and a child of theirs fell sick and so continued seventeen or eighteen weeks, and then died.

It was clearly a risky business to fall out with this family for when they did not reward their enemies with death, the Trevisards inflicted curious punishments. Thus, when Alice Trevisard was refused credit for a half-penny's worth of ale, she caused a full cask to fall to the ground and the ale in it to waste. Worse still was the fate of a woman whose father-in-law had quarrelled with the Trevisards. Her neck shrank so that her chin touched her breast and 'remaineth still in a very strange manner'.

Scapegoats

The Trevisards seem to have been blamed for almost everything which went wrong in Hardness. When the Cattle Pound was damaged by wind, Michael Trevisard had raised the storm; when Susan Tooker had an illness lasting seven weeks, it was because she had refused Peter Trevisard some beer; while when William Tompson came back to England after a year in a Spanish prison, it was remembered that he had once hit Alice Trevisard. All in all the Trevisards fulfilled a useful function as scapegoats.

The existence of local families as scapegoats can be discerned in the evidence given at witch trials in every country of western Europe. The social function of these families seems to have been an important, if unpleasant, one. They relieved the psychological tensions of small communities by being loaded with the frustrations, annoyances and guilts of the rest of the population.

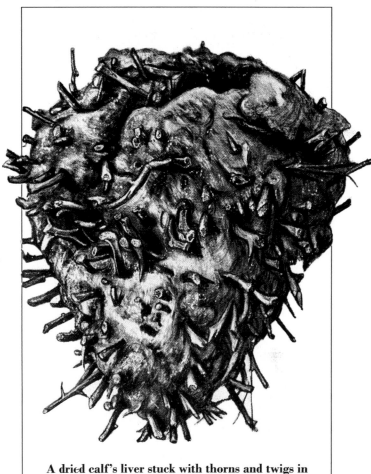

A dried calf's liver stuck with thorns and twigs in a Devonshire cottage. It was probably intended to cause the death of some enemy of a 'wise woman' or 'cunning man'.

Murder by means of the potions contained in the box held by one of these witches was portrayed by Goya as an offering to the demon bats who hover above.

Plague ointment

Witches were also made scapegoats for much greater calamities than broken beer casks, shrunken necks or imprisonment. It was they who were often blamed for crop failures and for the great epidemics of plague, the sweating sickness and other diseases which swept Europe until modern times.

At Berlin, in 1553, a mother who sought a missing child called at a neighbour's house where, so she said, she found the dismembered body of the infant being cooked in a large cauldron by two women. She called for help, the two women were arrested and, after torture, confessed that they had been performing a rite intended to result in an intense frost which would destroy the fruit crop.

The Italian physician Jerome Cardan described how, in 1536, the witches of Saluzzo spread the plague by sprinkling magical powder and applying a noxious ointment to the doors of houses. Forty people, one of them was the public hangman, were arrested for this, subjected to 'exquisite tortures' and executed.

To be a scapegoat has never been pleasant or safe.

In the 1580s the schoolmaster of the Scottish village of Saltpans was a certain John Fian, a man learned in the black arts as well as in those subjects which he taught his pupils.

One day Fian asked a pupil to bring him some of the pubic hair of his older sister. On the following night the boy, clearly very stupid or very obedient, attempted to comply. He crept to the bed of the sleeping girl, pulled back the coverlet, and tried to carry out his task. The girl awoke and called her mother. The boy, cross-questioned, explained his conduct and was given some hairs to take to the schoolmaster, but these were taken from the udder of one of the family's cows, not from the girl.

The mother, it is apparent, suspected Fian of planning to work love magic and a day or two later her beliefs were justified. For the unlucky schoolmaster was pursued throughout the village by the now lust-maddened cow which came 'leaping and dancing upon him . . . to the great admiration of all the townsmen of Saltpans'.

Fian certainly existed, but it is sure that this story, told in *Newes From Scotland* (1591), is apocryphal, for very similar tales had been in common circulation for centuries.

Coriander and cake

Nevertheless, the story presents clearly one of the key features of the 'love magic' (which would be more accurately termed 'lust magic') which was practised by village wise women, witches and sorcerers. It usually, although not invariably, involved the manipulation of substances, such as hair or physical secretions, derived from the body of the bewitched person.

Sometimes such manipulations seem harmless enough. Thus, a spell contained in a book of folk sorcery which was reprinted as recently as the 1960s instructs a woman how to gain the love of a man. She must take a hair from the man's head, a little coriander seed and 'some of the dust from beneath her own feet' and package them in cloth with a thread taken from the man's clothing. She must then hide the package in a place frequented by the man saying, as she does so, 'Anusin, Anusin, Atetin, Atetin, Atelin'.

Other spells of folk witchery were considerably more earthy. One called for a woman to get herself into a lather of sweat and to clean the sweat off with flour. This latter was to be mixed with ashes derived from burning hairs from every part of her body, egg and oil. The

A young sorceress anointing herself with ointments with the purpose of making herself sexually desirable to a particular man or men in general.

concoction was baked and served as a cake to the object of the witch's sexual desire.

The mirror of Venus

Mirrors have been associated with love goddesses since classical times and there survive details of a number of love spells involving the use of mirrors. One such, of which a number of variants are to be found in manuscript sources, began by the witch or sorcerer purchasing a hand mirror, preferably one backed with copper, the metal traditionally associated with Venus. The name of the subject of the spell and certain mystic characters were written on the back of the mirror, which was then taken to a spot where a dog and a bitch were likely to be encountered engaged in copulation. When the canine passions were at their height, the mirror was held so that the scene was reflected in it.

All this established a magical link between the sorcerer as the owner of the mirror, the victim of the spell whose name was on the mirror's back, and the abstract idea of copulation which had been absorbed magically into the mirror when it had reflected the dogs. The victim had only to glance into the mirror and the spell would exert the intended effects.

It all sounds very complex, but if both man and woman believed in the efficacy of love magic it probably worked.

A sheep's heart pierced with hawthorn twigs and nailed to the door of a Norfolk castle – possibly intended to kill, but more probably to induce love.

A 19th-century interpretation of the preparation of a love potion. Such potions often contained ingredients that were dangerous, such as cantharides, or derived from body fluids.

IMPOTENCE AND SATYRIASIS

Hugh of St Victor, a 12th-century theologian, defined black magic as 'the damnable arts of incantating demons and tying knots in laces'.

The last refers to what was commonly known as 'tying the points', a technique involving the use of knotted cords which sorcerers and witches employed in order to make men impotent. Such impotence could be general, the victim of the spell being unable to engage in any sort of sexual activity, or it could be more particular. In this case the man could not achieve erection with some special partner, most commonly his newly-married wife.

The frequency of such supposedly witchcraft-induced impotence was explained by some on the basis of the human genitals being 'inherently evil'. The authors of *The Hammer of the Witches* (*see* p. 33) asserted that God allows witches to have a particularly strong influence over 'the generative powers because they are more corrupt than other human powers'.

On its most basic level tying the points was a simple piece of imitative magic. The witch mentally identified a piece of string with the penis of her intended victim and tied a knot in it, thus magically preventing the free flow of blood and vital essences.

Most of those accused of making men impotent by 'tying the laces' made full confessions after they had been subjected to prolonged and painful torture.

Doctor Lambe, a Jacobean sorcerer renowned for his aphrodisiac potions, eventually was murdered by an angry London mob as he was leaving a theatre.

Sexual sorcery

More elaborate techniques than imitative magic were employed by many sorcerers and witches. If one proved a failure, other methods would be employed until success was achieved. Hollen, an Augustinian canon who wrote towards the end of the 15th century, claimed to know personally a woman who was an expert practitioner of this sexual sorcery. Hollen's acquaintance, who was probably a midwife who cast spells for some of her clients in return for money, had been employed by someone to bring about magically the separation of a married couple; presumably the client was the husband's mistress or the wife's lover.

The witch began by writing 'strange characters and devout words' on pieces of paper which she induced the husband and wife to sew into their clothing. This seems odd, but very probably the witch told the couple that she was giving them charms which would ensure good luck. Whatever the truth of the matter, the amulets did not achieve their purpose and the sorceress resorted to stronger magic, buying a great cheese, carving mystic symbols on its rind, and giving it to the couple as a present.

Either the couple did not like cheese and left it uneaten or the second spell was as ineffective as the first; certainly, reported Hollen, the couple remained on excellent terms.

The black chicken

At this stage the witch abandoned pure sorcery, the manipulation of material substances or objects for magical purposes, and involved herself in sinful *latria* (*see* p.31), by killing a black chicken and offering half of it to Satan 'with certain sacrificial rites'. The other half of the chicken was cooked and given to the married couple. This achieved the desired end and from that time forth, said Hollen, there arose between husband and wife 'the greatest hatred . . . so they could not bear to look at each other'.

Witches were reputed not only to be capable of magically causing male impotence but of inducing its opposite, a state of continuous penile erection. This curious condition seems to have held a certain fascination for some Renaissance writers on witchcraft and demonology and their treatises are replete with stories of tumescent male organs, most of them somewhat indecent. Such stories cannot, however, be totally written off as male sexual fantasies. Possibly some witches knew of dangerous drugs, such as cantharides, which can both kill and produce long lasting erection.

Those suspected of having employed witchcraft to disrupt the sexual lives of their neighbours were subjected to the indignity of being pricked with needles in order to find 'devil's marks' or insensible areas of skin.

DEMON LOVERS – THE INCUBUS

An astonished husband is warned by a bystander that at the very door of his home his wife is consorting with her demon lover.

Hector Boece, a 16th-century Scottish scholar, told a very odd story concerning a young girl of gentle blood whose family owned lands on the shores of the Moray Firth. The girl, against all the social customs of the time in which she lived, inexplicably refused offers of marriage from several noblemen who were rich, good looking and regarded with approval by her parents. Eventually, the parents demanded an explanation and their daughter confessed that she had no wish to marry because she had already lost her virginity to a lover, 'the best in the world'. Pressed for further details she added that she did not know her lover's name nor 'whence he came or whither he went'; from time to time he appeared, as though from nowhere, made love to her and vanished away.

Not surprisingly the parents found this story difficult to believe, and assuming that the girl was keeping her lover's identity secret for some reason of her own, determined to discover the truth by ordering their servants to keep a watch on her activities.

Violent lovemaking

Three days later a serving wench told them that the girl had shut herself in her chamber and that from it were coming the sounds of violent lovemaking. Accom-

panied by the domestic chaplain, whom Boece described as 'a most holy priest, skilled in the rituals of exorcism', the girl's parents rushed to the door of their daughter's room and broke it down. They saw 'in their daughter's embrace a monster horrible beyond description'. The priest immediately began to recite the opening verses of St John's Gospel. When he reached the Latin phrase which is translated as 'the Word was made Flesh and dwelt amongst us', recorded Boece:

> *. . . the evil demon gave a terrible cry, set fire to all the furniture of the room and vanished upwards, carrying with him the roof of the bedroom. The girl . . . [later] gave birth to a monster of utterly loathsome appearance . . .*

A demon lover of this sort, i.e., one who took on the illusory appearance of a male human being and mated with women, was known as an *incubus*, this term being derived from the Latin word *incubo* and literally meaning 'burden' or 'weight'. It seems to have become applied to supposed nonhuman lovers, because it was thought that nightmares involving a feeling of weight on the chest were the consequence of the erotic attentions of demons of the night.

As is made apparent by the claws upon the feet and hands of this woman's lover, he is an incubus luring her to destruction.

A woman, perhaps against her will, engages in perverted sexual congress with the demon who officiates at the ceremonies of the Witches' Sabbath.

Watchers and fauns

Boece's report that the sexual union of a girl with a fiend had resulted in the birth of a monster reflected a very ancient tradition, and the belief in the possibility of supernatural beings – gods, angels, or demons – fathering the children of mortal women is probably almost as old as humanity itself. Thus, many of the heroes of classical legend were regarded as having been, quite literally, half divine and the Watchers of Jewish legend (*see* p.15) were reputed to have fathered giants.

It was not only gods and angels but far inferior spirit entities who were believed to procreate half-human children. Thus, in the 5th century St Augustine referred to the sexual activities of the fauns and satyrs, nature spirits whose forms were a blend of man and goat. He wrote that:

Many persons say that they have had the experience, or have heard from such as have had the experience, that the satyrs and fauns, whom the common people call incubi, have presented themselves before women and sought and procured intercourse with them.

Similarly, witches were reputed to give birth to the children of demons. But how, it was asked, could devils, whose seeming physical bodies were illusory, procreate children. The answer given is only explicable if one understands the nature of the *succubus*.

DEMON LOVERS – THE SUCCUBUS

The erotic dreams of both men and women, particularly when such dreams resulted in sexual climax, were thought to be caused by the activities of, respectively, succubi and incubi.

A *succubus* was defined as a demon which took on the illusory appearance of a woman and had relationships with men.

Reports of the activities of these creatures surprisingly were common in the Middle Ages and the Renaissance and, generally, it was accepted that the physical temptations and satisfactions they offered to unwary men sometimes led the latter into the dark world of witchcraft. Thus, the 16th-century author, Nicolas Remy, told of a herdsman found guilty of witchcraft who, when asked how he had first fallen into the company of witches, explained that he had been corrupted by a *succubus*. The herdsman said that he had fallen passionately in love with a dairymaid who, alas, did not return his affection. One day when he was, in his own words, 'burning with desire in his solitary pasturage' he saw what at first he took for the person of his beloved hiding behind a bush. He ran to her, made violent advances, and was repulsed. After a while, however, the 'dairymaid' – in reality a demon who had assumed the girl's appearance – allowed the herdsman to do with her body as he would on condition that he 'acknowledged her as his Mistress and behaved to her as though she were God Himself'. The herdsman would appear to have found his demon coupling physically satisfying, but found that 'she so possessed me from that time I have been subject to no will but hers'.

Cold baths

One line of defence against the erotic wiles of demons manifesting as *succubi* was the employment of prayer, fasting and other religious devotions. At some time, around the year 1500, the Bishop of Aberdeen is recorded as having successfully prescribed such remedies for a young man who approached him for spiritual advice. For many months, complained the young man, he had been pestered by a *succubus* who came to him by night and either coaxed or forced him into a sexual embrace which lasted until the break of day. The Bishop ordered the victim to engage in devout prayer and austerity. Perhaps this was a 16th-century version of the regime of 'cold baths and low diet' which Victorian physicians ordered to be imposed on boys suspected of 'solitary vice', i.e., masturbation. Certainly it seems to have been successful, for the chronicler who told the story recorded that 'after a few days the young man was delivered from the succubus devil'.

The latrines of superstition

Sometimes, however, those following a life of religious devotion found their prayers of little efficacy against the wiles of *succubi*. Thus, for example, towards the end of the last century the French writer, J.K. Huysmans, claimed to have been attacked by a *succubus* whilst staying in a monastery.

Huysmans, a novelist of distinction who had at one time been an unbeliever but was in process of returning to the Catholic Church, was on a short monastic retreat. This was intended as a spiritual antidote to the psychological effects of the several years he had spent in what he himself called 'the latrines of superstition' – a reference to his contacts with the sometimes sinister subculture of 19th-century Parisian occultism.

One night, lying on his hard monastic bed, Huysmans awoke from the climax of an erotic dream to see a *succubus* vanishing away. That it had taken a physical form and was not illusory was apparent, Huysmans said, from the appearance of the sheets he had shared with the demon. Huysmans' dream had ended with an intense ejaculation. According to demonologists, the fruits of such *succubi*-induced climaxes were borne away by demons who then, taking on the forms of *incubi*, used them to fertilize human women.

Succubi, like the wood nymphs of classical times and the bloodsucking nightriders of Germanic legend, were reputed in some places to sit in trees, awaiting potential victims.

Gustav Klimt's portrayal of a sexually-aware young witch conveys all the deadly charm of the demon in female form known as the succubus.

A folk belief which was still alive in the Meon Hills of Shakespeare's Warwickshire until the middle of the last century concerned the Hell Hounds. These were seen, it was claimed, on either Christmas Eve or New Year's Eve and took the form of a pack of fox hounds, different from any other pack only in that it hunted during the hours of darkness and was accompanied by but a single horseman. This solitary hunter and his pack could be dangerous. If the man spoke to those he encountered – perhaps enquiring the way to some village, or asking that a gate should be barred after the passage of himself and his dogs – it was essential that he should be disregarded. For anyone who spoke to, or helped in any way, the lone horseman and his Hell Hounds would never again be seen in the world of men. Instead he would be condemned to roam the cold spaces of ghostland until the Day of Judgement.

The eyes of cats have been described as 'windows looking out upon another world'. Certainly cats have always been associated with the supernatural since their first domestication.

A hell hound such as this one has often been associated with black magic and its practitioners. Faust was believed to have had one, as was Cornelius Agrippa.

Gabriel Ratchets

By the 19th century the Master of the Hell Hounds of the Meon Hills was regarded as a ghost, the spirit of a once living man. There was no exact agreement on either the identity of the ghostly horseman or the reason for which he had been condemned to hunt through the night. Some said he was a huntsman who, 100 years before, had tormented his hounds and been torn to pieces by them. Others said that he was a sinner who had defied the law of God by hunting on a Sunday. However, 300 years earlier the huntsman would unquestionably have been regarded as Satan himself and his dogs as subsidiary demons, literally Hell Hounds.

A belief in Satan as hunter of the night was once common throughout most of western Europe. In Icelandic folk belief, the demons who served the Devil's hunt in either animal or human shape were known as 'the Yule Host', in Germany as 'the Angry Host', in different regions of France as the *Chasse Artu* and *Chasse Maccabei*, in the west of England as 'the Wisht Hounds', and in Yorkshire as the 'Gabriel Ratchets'.

The last name, which survived in folk traditions which were still alive towards the end of the last century, is particularly interesting for it shows the antiquity of the belief. 'Gabriel' has nothing to do with the angel Gabriel but is a corruption of the medieval word *gabares*, meaning a corpse. Similarly, ratchet is a corruption of *rache*, meaning a dog which hunts by scent, so the Gabriel Ratchets were 'corpse hounds'.

Seven whistlers

The Devil and his demon hounds were believed to be the familiar companions of witches and there is some reason to believe that they are a Christianized version of the Teutonic belief in the wild hunt led by the god Wotan.

In English folk belief the legend of the wild hunt not only became blended with the idea of witches and their imps flying to the Sabbath but also with a belief in the seven whistlers, i.e., the leaders of a night-flying flock which were seemingly birds but were in truth the souls of those who have died unhappily and were condemned to wander the upper air until the end of time. Sometimes these unhappy souls were believed to be unbaptized children and their seven leaders, the whistlers, those men who had crucified Christ. In other versions of the story, they were identified with drowned sailors, or miners who had died in accidents.

It was not only demons who manifested themselves as hounds. Witches were believed to follow the same course – and some of them were burned for it.

'Herne the Hunter', the antlered and sinister huntsman, of whom sightings are occasionally still reported in the park around Windsor Castle, is another figure associated with the Wild Hunt.

GLAMOUR AND SHAPE CHANGING

A country midwife was summoned one night from her bed by a richly dressed horseman who told her that her services were required urgently by the wife of a nobleman. Riding pillion behind the horseman – a familiar mode of country travel until the 18th century – she was taken through unfamiliar roads to a great house ablaze with light.

The nobleman met the couple at the door and took the midwife to the room in which his wife lay. Shortly afterwards the lady was delivered of a son. The midwife was then handed a box of ointment and instructed to anoint the child's face with it. She was told, however, that the substance was so precious that it must be applied with a cloth, so that none of it should touch her own skin.

As the midwife applied the unguent her left eye began to itch. Without thinking she dabbed at it with the cloth she held and the scene before her immediately changed. The magnificent chamber in which the birth had taken place vanished from sight and now appeared to be a rocky cave. The beautiful noblewoman became a toothless witch, her husband a black demon and their child a wizened imp.

Magical deception

Variants of this folk tale have been collected over wide areas of the British Isles and Continental Europe. In some versions of the tale the family encountered by the midwife are trolls, dwarfs or elves rather than witches and demons, but in essence the same point is made – witches and other supernatural beings have the ability to create illusions, to deceive ordinary human beings by magically presenting things as other than they really are. Illusions of this type were known as 'glamour', the original meaning of this word, and a 'glamorous

Our ancestors were never quite sure of the true identity of those seeming humans they encountered on heaths and in forests. This old hag *may* be a witch, a spirit, or even the Queen of Faery.

Glamour, in its original sense of illusion and even deception, has always been associated with ritual magic. Here the French occultist Dr Encausse (Papus) represented both the physical appearance and the supposed reality of ceremony.

woman' would have been one who had an 'illusory' beauty.

A particular form of glamour was shape changing, the supposed ability of witches to create the illusion that they had changed into animals. In popular folk belief such changes were regarded as genuinely having been made – the witch or sorcerer was thought to have become a real animal – but the Church thought otherwise, teaching that a human soul, even that of a witch, cannot occupy the body of a beast. To think the contrary was regarded as a gross doctrinal error. In the words of an Italian theologian and demonologist:

> . . . no one must let himself think that a man can really be transformed into an animal, or an animal into a man. These are magical portents and illusions, having the form but not the substance of those things which they present to our sight.

Curiously enough, however, the demonologists believed that harm done to the animal phantasm of a witch was transmitted to that same witch's human body.

Witch cats

Nicolas Remy, a 16th-century judge who sent many men and women to the stake said that almost all the witches he had encountered habitually turned themselves into cats 'when they wished to enter other people's houses'.

A 16th-century labourer in the Italian city of Ferrara made a sworn statement concerning his experience of such a witch cat. He and his wife had seen a large cat approach their son. They kept shooing it away but the cat insistently returned until, beaten with a stick, it

The frightful monsters with whom witches consorted might, through the employment of magical glamour, appear to outsiders as no more than domestic animals.

seemed 'broken and bruised'. Immediately afterwards a neighbour who practised as a healing wise woman, but was suspected of sorcery, took to her bed, covered from head to foot with great wounds and bruises. Suspicion of witchcraft was considered as having been proved.

Similar cases were reported at around the same time from almost every part of western Europe – not only injured cats but dogs, hares and even giant toads were revealed as disguised witches.

A Russian chieftain of the 16th century heard reports that one of his peasant subjects could change himself into a wolf whenever he wished to do so. He summoned the man before him and, taking the precaution of having the man securely chained, ordered him to transform himself into a wolf.

The peasant said he would do so willingly but lacked the power unless he was alone. He was allowed to go, still chained, into the next room from which he came bounding back as a wolf 'to the astonishment of all present'. The peasant's obedience did him no good at all, for the ferocious dogs kept by the chieftain attacked the intruding wolf and tore him to pieces.

Similar tales are told in almost every part of the world – werewolf stories are the most common but there are also accounts of weretigers, werepanthers and even werehyenas.

Master of the forest

The Church's demonologists regarded the supposed transformation of men into wolves as being mere

The ancient legend of lycanthropy – man or woman transformed into ravening wolf – still exerts its magic on the filmgoers of the 1980s.

Some of those executed as werewolves, such as the man depicted here, unquestionably were guilty of mass murder and were criminally insane individuals suffering from delusions of lycanthropy.

Normally wolves do not attack human beings and usually they hunt in packs. Any wolf which, in isolation from others, attacked a traveller consequently was suspected of being supernatural.

glamour, as illusory as other varieties of shape changing, and thus witchcraft. A theologian explained that Satan:

> *. . . surrounds a witch with an aerial effigy . . . each part of which fits on to the correspondent part of the witch's body, head to head, mouth to mouth, belly to belly, foot to foot, and arm to arm . . .*

Witches, said the same theologian, use unguents and magical incantations seemingly to change into wolves but, although they leave the wolf footprints upon the ground as they pass, they are still human.

The use of such an ointment was a feature of the werewolf confession made by Jean Grenier, a 13-year-old boy who was tried at Bordeaux in 1603. Grenier was almost certainly a deeply unhappy boy – his parents ill treated him and he gained a meagre living by rural casual labour and beggary – who got into trouble by attempting to impress other children with lying stories. Certainly, there is strong evidence that he boasted to other children that at times he had turned into a wolf and killed dogs and, on one occasion, a young girl.

Some time afterwards a young girl claimed to have been attacked by a wolf or dog which, so she said, she recognized as Grenier. The boy was arrested, charged and tried. In evidence he admitted to having met a

being whom he called 'The Master of the Forest' who had given him an ointment and a wolfskin cloak which enabled him to change his shape. He also confessed to killing and eating several young children.

Amazingly enough he was not sent to the stake. The judge, either exceptionally humane or suspecting the boy was insane, said he thought it better 'to save a soul for God than consider it lost' and ordered Jean to spend the rest of his life in a monastery.

Wolf magic

A desire to become a werewolf seems an odd ambition for even the most perverse witch or sorcerer to entertain, but according to 16th and 17-century sources some human beings carried out complicated magical rites in order to achieve it. Such ceremonies involved the raising of demons, as well as the preparation and 'consecration' of a wolfskin belt. This was believed to be imbued thus with the power of transformation. According to some French accounts, such a belt was quite as effective as wolfskin if it was made from the tanned skin of an executed criminal, preferably a witch.

According to folk belief there were simpler methods of becoming a werewolf. Drinking water from a wolf's pawprint, eating the roasted flesh of a rabid wolf and sleeping in the light of a full moon when it fell upon a Friday were all considered effective.

Witches were believed capable of inflicting the households of those against whom they bore a grudge with a variety of annoyances ranging from such petty irritations as mysterious noises to the outbreak of fire destroying property and life.

On one occasion a witch and her demon lover, an *incubus* with whom she was said to have had a sexual relationship over a period of 14 years, were held responsible for the destruction of an entire 'town' – in present day terms a large village. This was Schiltach, in Switzerland, which was consumed by fire in the spring of 1533.

The demon drummer of Tedworth (now Tadworth) was believed to have the mysterious witch power of being in two places at once. When in gaol he was seen simultaneously by Jarvis Matcham 100 miles away.

The whistling demon

The affair began, said popular report, with an outbreak of mysterious whistling in a particular house, the master of which could find neither the whistler nor be quite sure exactly from which part of the house the whistling was coming. It was significant, however, that the noise seemed to be centred on the smoke chamber, a small room built around, and open to, the main chimney of the house in which hams and other meats were hung for smoking.

The master of the house called in two local priests, who decided that the whistler was a demon and carried out an exorcism. This was quite ineffective, so the priests threatened to offer up celebrations of the Mass with the intention of making the hellish whistler depart to its own place. The demon was unimpressed and told the priests that it 'cared nothing for their menaces'. It is to be presumed that the demon spoke through the mouth of someone it had possessed temporarily, and there is little doubt that this person was the witch who possessed a demon lover. For some time afterwards that woman was carried into the air by the whistling demon and set down in the smoke chamber where she upset a jar. This started a blaze, said the account supplied by a local magistrate, which was of such intensity 'that the whole town was burned down within one hour'.

It seems improbable that any supernatural factors were truly involved in the destruction of Schiltach. The supposed witch, almost certainly a mentally unbalanced servant in the house in which the blaze started, had begun by engaging in practical jokes involving whistling, had gone on to pretend (or have the delusion) that she was possessed by a demon lover, and, finally, had committed arson.

Strange tumults

It is not so easy to find an explanation of the demon drumming which troubled the house of an English gentleman, Mr Mompesson of Tedworth, in the early 1660s.

Mr Mompesson's troubles began with the arrival in the area of a vagrant drummer named William Drury, a discharged soldier who carried a pass authorizing him to beg. This proved to be forged, and the drum was confiscated. A month later Mr Mompesson's house, in which the drum had been deposited, began to suffer nightly disturbances – 'great knockings' were heard on the walls, strange tumults were heard in the air, and the noise of drumming filled the house.

The centre of the noises was the room containing the drum and the latter was destroyed. This had no effect and the nuisances increased. The drumming became more prolonged, the noise of clinking money was heard and, oddest of all, Mr Mompesson's horse was found one morning with its hind legs stuffed into its mouth.

The drummer had made his way to Gloucester where he was jailed for theft. Word of happenings at Mompesson's house reached him and he is reported to have commented 'I have plagued him and he shall never be quiet till he hath made me satisfaction for taking away my drum'. He was charged with witchcraft and aquitted, but transported for theft.

The drumming ceased.

Joseph Glanvil, scholar and theologian, was a firm believer in the reality of witchcraft and gave an account of a personal encounter with the demon drummer in his *Saducissmus Triumphatus.*

Christina Rossetti, sister of the founder of the group of painters known as the Pre-Raphaelite Brotherhood, was well aware of the ancient belief that the Fairy Queen's subjects were not always benevolent.

Nothing could appear more innocent than the gossamer frail fairies portrayed in children's picture books or the delicate elves described in accounts given by some present day clairvoyants.

Yet, there was an eerie and baneful element in traditional fairy lore. Fairies were, in fact, the friends of witches and were themselves, so it was said, sometimes guilty of crimes almost identical with those committed by the blackest of sorcerers. In Scotland, for example, it was believed that witches were companions of the *bhaobhan sidhe*, which in Gaelic means something like 'vampire fairies'. As late as the last century stories concerning the unpleasant activities of these lovely but evil creatures were told and half believed by Gaelic speaking Highland crofters.

Green ladies

One such tale concerned four hunters in Ross who took shelter for the night in a bothy, a primitive hut used as temporary accommodation by shepherds and cowherds, lighted a fire and began to talk longingly of their sweethearts. Suddenly, there entered four lovely girls clad entirely in green and three of the hunters began to dance with them while the fourth man sang. As the dance became wilder the singer became aware that great drops of blood were appearing, as though from nowhere, upon the ground. Terrified, the singer ran out into the night and hid in thick undergrowth until dawn when, trembling with fright, he crept back into the bothy. The ladies had vanished as mysteriously as they had appeared but upon the ground lay the three dancers, lifeless and utterly drained of blood.

It seems apparent that the green ladies, the vampire fairies of Celtic folklore, are in essence identical with Germanic nightriders who devoured the entrails of men (*see* p.22) and the witches, *striges*, of classical times.

Richard Dadd, who spent many years in a lunatic asylum after he had murdered his own father, admirably conveyed the more sinister aspects of fairy lore in his *Fairy Feller's Master-Stroke*.

Seed of the proud angel

The fairies of Celtic and Norse folklore often were identified with the fallen angels who had shared in Satan's rebellion against God or, alternatively, with the half-human children of those angels. A rhyme current in the Hebrides during the last century had the fairy folk boldly proclaiming:

Not of the seed of Adam are we,
Nor is Abraham our father,
But of the seed of the proud angel
Driven forth from heaven.

In other words, the fairies were the children of Satan and, as such, demons. This view was strongly held amongst some groups of believers in witchcraft, but others took a more charitable view and regarded the subjects of the Queen of Faery as neither totally good nor morally evil. Thus, Robert Kirke, a 17th-century

Scottish minister, the author of an eccentric treatise entitled *The Secret Commonwealth of Elves*, claimed that fairies were 'of a middle nature betwixt man and Angel', while according to one Irish tradition fairies are the innocent, deluded subjects of Satan rather than his accomplices.

Oddly enough, this idea that there exists a class of semi-demons, neither wholly bad nor wholly good, was revived in the last century by Cardinal Newman, who admitted to a belief in spirits who were '. . . neither in heaven nor in hell; partially fallen, capricious, wayward; noble or crafty, benevolent or malicious as the case might be'.

Probably it was their reputation as beings who were subject at least partially to Lucifer that was responsible for the belief that fairies stole human children, taking unattended babes from their cradles and substituting creatures of their own begetting. The stolen children were handed over, so it was believed, to Satan who longed for human souls to people his dark kingdom.

To fall asleep upon a 'fairy mound' or tumulus was considered to be foolhardy in the extreme, for the sleeper's mind could become subject to malignant fairy impostures.

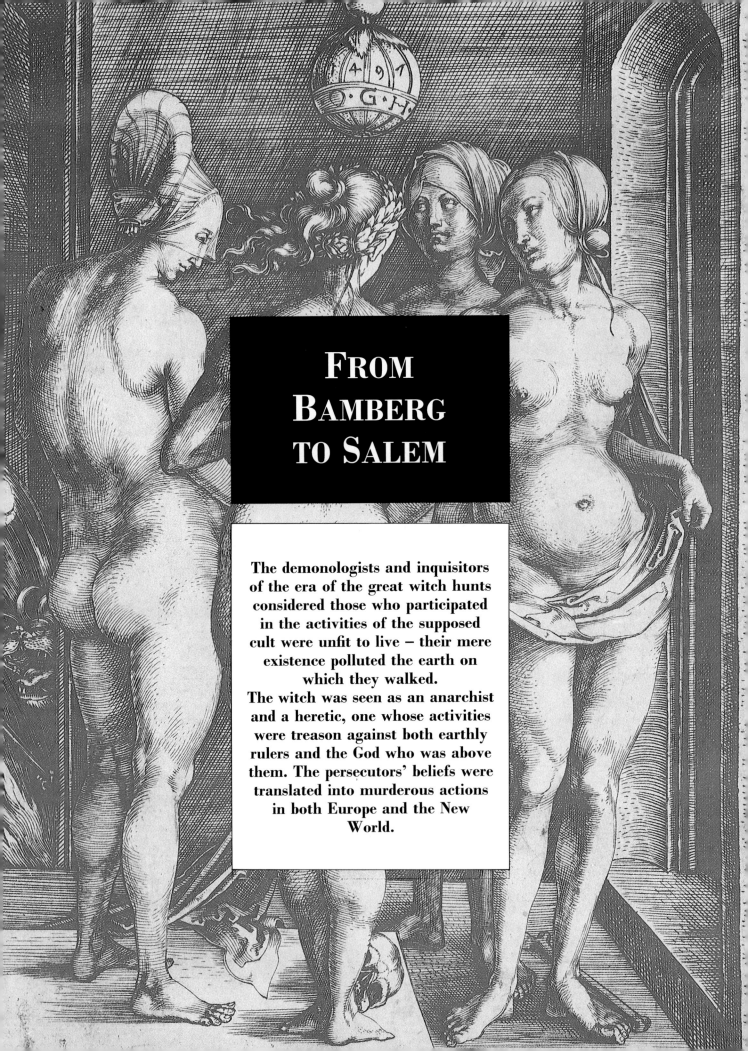

FROM BAMBERG TO SALEM

The demonologists and inquisitors of the era of the great witch hunts considered those who participated in the activities of the supposed cult were unfit to live – their mere existence polluted the earth on which they walked.

The witch was seen as an anarchist and a heretic, one whose activities were treason against both earthly rulers and the God who was above them. The persecutors' beliefs were translated into murderous actions in both Europe and the New World.

TERROR AT BAMBERG

Bamberg, a small state ruled by a Prince Bishop, witnessed the cruellest of all the witch persecutions which took place in the German-speaking world. There was a long tradition of supposed witchcraft amongst the subjects of the Prince Bishop and an equally strong tradition of submitting those accused of this offence to prolonged tortures. It was during the 1620s, however, that the Bamberg persecution reached its peak and during that decade something like 600 people were tortured and executed.

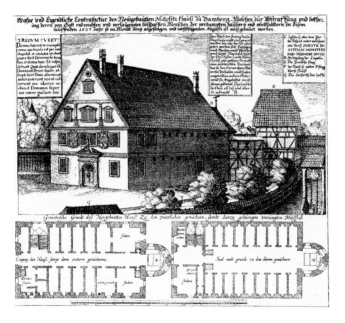

No one who was subjected to the tortures inflicted in the Bamberg Witch Prison failed to confess to attendance at the Sabbath and other crimes.

The Witches' House

Economic and social factors played some part in the genesis of the Bamberg persecutions. There were tensions resulting from religious factors and there is no doubt that some people had a vested financial interest in the instigation and continuation of witch hunts. These latter included, for example, a number of ecclesiastical lawyers. Nevertheless, it is difficult to draw any other conclusion than that the quite exceptional ferocity of the persecutions of the 1620s directly

resulted from the greed and obsessional concern with the witchcraft of one man, the Prince Bishop von Dornheim, who ruled the state from 1623 until 1632.

Von Dornheim established an efficient witch-hunting bureaucracy which was led by a suffragan bishop, Friedrich Forner, and was staffed on its highest levels by lawyers, employed a number of full-time torturers and executioners, and used informers in a way reminiscent of the Gestapo three centuries later. The centre of the witch hunters' activities was a special prison, the Hexenhaus – 'Witches' House' – where torture was used so effectively that not one of those imprisoned there failed to confess to participation in witchcraft.

Popular sympathy

It was unsafe for anyone to suggest that the slightest mercy should be shown to those accused of witchcraft. Anyone who did would himself almost certainly fall under suspicion. Thus, the Vice-Chancellor of the diocese, Dr Haan, who was thought to have shown some tendency to leniency, was denounced as a witch and burned with his wife and daughter.

Under torture Dr Haan not only had admitted to attendance at the Witches' Sabbath but named five of the leading burgomasters of the Prince Bishopric as being amongst his fellow Devil worshippers. The five men, respected and wealthy, were immediately arrested and 'questioned'.

The nature of the questioning to which they were submitted was made clear in a passage from a letter which one of them, Johannes Junius, smuggled out: 'And then came . . . the executioner and put the thumbscrews on me . . . so that the blood spurted . . . so that for four weeks I could not use my hands, as you can see from my writing'. It was impossible to resist such torments and Junius, having confessed to attending the Witches' Sabbath, desecrating the consecrated host and having sexual relations with a *succubus*, was sent to the stake.

Refugees from the Bamberg holocaust appealed to the Emperor, the Prince Bishop's overlord, who had been told already by his confessor that victims of the hunt were popularly regarded as innocent and worthy of sympathy. The Emperor ordered that, in future, the property of those accused should not be confiscated. The persecution immediately slackened and, within two years, was over.

The accusations made at Bamberg in the 1620s bore a very marked resemblance to those made almost two centuries earlier in Arras, the important mercantile city which was the centre of the first great witch persecution of the 15th century.

The Arras witch hunt had its origins at Langres in the year 1459 when a hermit, probably suspected of heresy, was arrested, tortured and sent to the stake. Under torture, the hermit admitted to attendance at the Sabbath and named as his companions a young prostitute of Douai and an elderly poet of Arras. In spite of the improbability of these accusations – the poet was well-known for his poems in praise of the Blessed Virgin – the prostitute and poet were both arrested, tortured, confessed to witchcraft and named others as accomplices. These latter were arrested,

French heretics who followed the teachings of Peter of Waldo (known as 'Waldensians' or 'Vaudois') were accused of worshipping Lucifer under the form of a goat. In course of time such accusations also were made against witches.

French witches were believed to have the power of inducing dancing mania in their victims. According to legend the hangman of Aix and his wife were subjected in this way.

named others who also were arrested, and so on, like some ghastly pyramid-selling operation. As the cycle of arrests, confessions, denunciations, and more arrests became fully established, it began to exert a harmful influence on the commercial life of the city, a trading and manufacturing centre of great importance. For no one could be sure that a merchant of Arras would not be seized at a moment's notice, found guilty of witchcraft and have his entire wealth confiscated. Consequently, no outsider would extend credit to such a merchant.

Bishops and Cardinals

The persecution was conducted by the Arras inquisitor, who acted under the instructions of two fanatical Dominican friars, Jean, titular Bishop of Beirut and deputy for the Bishop of Arras, and Jacques du Boys, Dean of the general chapter of the Order of Preachers.

The two Dominicans shared some curious opinions –

that many Bishops and even Cardinals practised witchcraft, that one third of the entire population of Christian Europe were secret witches, and that anyone who opposed the burning of a witch thus proved himself to be a worshipper of Satan.

The Church service which preceded the first mass burning of the Arras persecution demonstrated the methods which had been used to obtain confessions without recourse to prolonged torture. At the service, at which all the accused witches were present, the inquisitor read out a description of the blasphemies and perversions allegedly practised at the Witches' Sabbath and asked those convicted to confirm the accuracy of the description. All did so, but when, at the end of the service, they were handed over for burning at the stake they retracted what they had said.

Doctors and heralds

Bound to the stakes at which they were to die, the condemned witches called out to those they knew in the watching crowd. They had never, they protested, attended the Sabbath, and had only been induced to say they had done so by means of torture and lying promises – they had been assured that if they confessed their only penance would be an obligation to go on a short pilgrimage.

Eventually, the Duke of Burgundy, feudal overlord of Arras, intervened and, after consultation with the doctors of Louvain, theologians whose learning was renowned throughout western Europe, he decreed that his heralds must be present at all future interrogations. This clear hint of ducal disapproval was enough for the inquisitors and, in spite of pressures exerted by the Dominicans who had initiated the persecution, arrests stopped immediately. The trials dragged on for a time, although most of the penalties imposed were fairly light, and did not cease until after the *Parlement* of Paris commenced to investigate the affair.

The investigation continued for 30 years but, eventually, those condemned were exonerated posthumously and a memorial to them erected on the site at which they had died, protesting their innocence as the flames rose around them.

An almost dualistic philosophy is expressed in this 15th-century miniature. On the left is the dark world of witches and demons, on the right that of angels and saints; humanity must make its choice.

BASQUE WITCHCRAFT

The lands bordering the Bay of Biscay and the Pyrenees – the kingdom of Navarre, the Asturias and the Basque country – had a long tradition of witch hunts and persecutions. Thus, for example, in 1527 two young girls, aged nine and eleven, appeared before a court in Pamplona and confessed to the usual abominable crimes. They were pardoned in return for their cooperation in securing the arrest of other witches whom they claimed they could recognize by a mystic sign; all witches, they said, had marks resembling frogs' feet in their eyes. The judge accepted this story and, accompanied by 50 armed soldiers and the two little girls, set out on a witch hunting expedition which resulted in the arrest and condemnation of 100 or so supposed sorcerers.

Similar childish denunciations were a feature of the witch persecution which took place at Vizcaya in 1555 and also in the following year. Those accused admitted to all the usual offences. They had flown through the air with the aid of ointments, they had harmed men and crops, they had worshipped Satan under the form of a black horse, and so on. Interestingly enough, none of those who confessed were executed; the judge, from motives of either scepticism or humanity sentenced none of them for more than a severe flogging.

While the stake was the usual punishment for witches and heretics in the dominions of the King of Spain, drowning was sometimes substituted – partial drowning sometimes was used as a means of extracting confessions from those accused.

Many of the village priests of the Basque regions were 'ordained peasants' of lax morality and little learning. This led one inquisitor to assert that many of them associated with witches such as those depicted here.

Sorcerers' soups

For some reason, not easily explainable, the years 1609–11 were marked by persecutions of exceptional severity and extent. It is almost as if there were outbreaks of mass hysteria in which judges were swept along, almost against their will, by a tide of popular feeling and prejudice.

A trial held at Logrono during this period indicates the sheer number of people supposed to have been involved in witchcraft. For of those who made full confessions, over 1,300 were children, the youngest aged six, the oldest fourteen.

Some years after the Logrono trial one of the judges, an inquisitor named Salazar y Frias who had become sceptical of the truth of the evidence he had heard, carried out a detailed analysis of the confessions made by the children. He found they were full of inconsistencies which revealed them to be lies or fantasies and came to the conclusion that he and his fellow judges had been woefully credulous. An exceptionally honest man, he admitted that he himself had been guilty of putting undue pressure on witnesses.

Salazar y Frias was very thorough in his investigations. He had 'witches' ointments' (which he rudely referred to as 'sorcerers' soups') manufactured according to the prescriptions given in confessions and applied them to animals without effect. On the date of a witch festival he sent observers to an isolated place where the Sabbath was alleged to take place and they witnessed nothing out of the ordinary.

Credulity

The scepticism of the Spaniard Salazar y Frias was, alas, in marked contrast to the credulous and murderous zeal of the French judge Pierre de Lancre who, in 1609–10, quite ignorant of the Basque language and believing that those who spoke it were all half-pagan barbarians, managed to reduce Navarre and the Basque provinces under French rule to a state of mindless terror.

In a book he published in 1612 de Lancre made the amazing claim that the majority of priests in parts of Navarre were witches. He told how he had induced one elderly priest to confess, following which event 'there was no longer hesitation in accusing priests' and 'innocent children . . . bore testimony to seeing them at the Sabbath'.

De Lancre's book sold widely and helped spark off further persecutions. For almost three centuries Salazar y Frias's careful report gathered dust in the archives of Spain.

In the Basque regions on both sides of the Pyrenees there were many survivals of ancient pagan practices. Inquisitors often interpreted participation in these as evidence of heresy or witchcraft.

REGINALD SCOT

Reading 16th and 17th-century treatises on witchcraft soon becomes a wearisome task. The first amusement at the improbable stories recounted as fact turns to boredom, and even disgust, when it is remembered that men and women suffered torture and death because learned theologians were credulous enough to believe that human beings flew through the air on broomsticks or sailed the sea in eggshells.

It is a relief to turn from such closely printed pages of scholarly gullibility to *The Discoverie of Witchcraft* (1584), a book written by Reginald Scot, a Kentish landowner who had no great pretensions to learning but was possessed of an abounding common sense.

Superstitious nonsense

Scot's book, the writing of which was almost certainly inspired by the author's disgust at the quality of the evidence which was accepted as reliable at the St Osyth witch trial of 1582, was a bold statement of personal scepticism. As far as Scot was concerned, there was nothing supernatural about witchcraft. It was true, he said, that there were people who believed they could heal or kill by the use of magic spells, but their beliefs were superstitious nonsense which no sensible person should take seriously. The claims made by some to have seen witches performing the impossible, such as flying

Scot was influenced deeply by the writings of Cornelius Agrippa, author of three volumes devoted to occult philosophy who, nevertheless, was a sceptic as regards witchcraft.

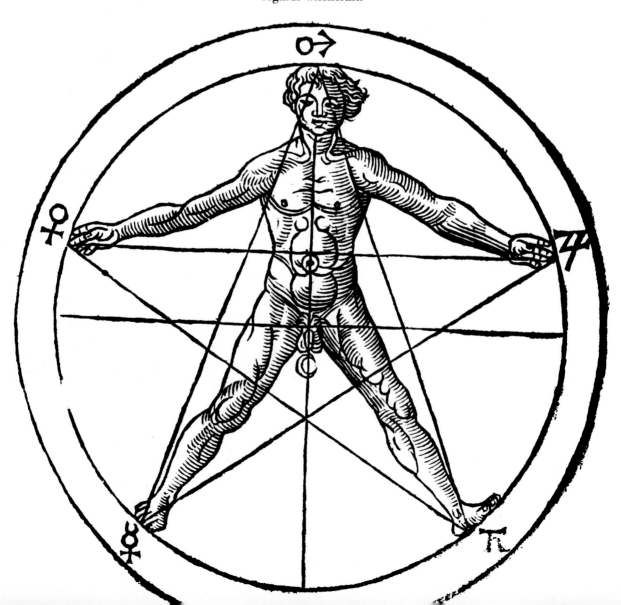

through the air, were rejected with equal contempt. Such claims, asserted Scot, were either fraudulent, mistaken or delusionary, a product of addled wits.

Scot's scepticism enraged many of his contemporaries, who regarded his book as 'atheistical', and it was not altogether original, for it had been anticipated by two European authors, to whom Scot referred with considerable respect. These were Cornelius Agrippa (1486–1535) who wrote about ritual magic, and probably practised it, but was doubtful of the reality of witchcraft, and Johannes Wier (1515–68). Wier, a physician whose knowledge of mental illness was considerable – at least one medical historian has referred to him as 'the father of psychiatry' – believed in demons and in the 'possibility' of witchcraft. He held, however, that most accusations of bewitchment were the product of fraud or mental illness. He wrote:

. . . uninformed and unskilled physicians relegate all the incurable diseases . . . to witchcraft . . . In all such cases a good doctor is to be consulted because . . . in no domain of human life are human passions so freely at play as in this one . . . these passions being superstition, rage, hate and malice.

The 16th century was not a good time in which to express scepticism. Wier's rationalism induced some

As Scot pointed out in the *Discoverie*, poor and elderly women, such as the one depicted here, were often village scapegoats – the subjects of witchcraft accusations.

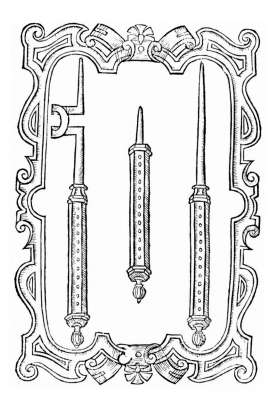

In his *Discoverie of Witchcraft*, Reginald Scot explained how illusionists performed some of their tricks. Simple people believed that such tricks as 'driving a bodkin through the head' were evidence of supernatural powers.

people to suspect him of witchcraft. Cornelius Agrippa was denounced as a sorcerer, and Scot was abused for his atheism.

The verdict of history

Scot's *Discoverie*, published in plain English instead of scholarly Latin, enjoyed a wide readership in spite of the abuse heaped upon its author. One reader of the book was Shakespeare, who seems to have drawn upon it for his portrayal of the witches in *Macbeth*.

Scot's book drew several angry replies from convinced believers in the reality of witchcraft. The first of these was published in 1587 by George Gifford, a Puritan minister renowned for his preaching, and was entitled *Discourse of the Subtle Practices of Devils by Witches and Sorcerers*. Another such reply was penned by William Perkins, a theologian whose ideas influenced those who conducted the Salem witch hunt of 1692. But Scot's fiercest and best-known opponent was King James VI of Scotland, later King James I of England, who not only attacked Scot in his *Demonology* (1597), but on his ascent to the English throne ordered copies of the *Discoverie* to be burned.

Eventually, however, Scot's ideas were to triumph over those of the witch hunters. History's verdict was to be in favour of the Kentish squire, not King James.

Isobel Gowdie's voluntary confession of witchcraft, one component of which is illustrated here, seems to have owed more to fantasy and mental illness than to genuine involvement in black magic.

Witchcraft trials were numerous in Scotland between 1450 and the end of the 17th century. Great importance has been given to two of them by those anxious to show that an organized cult existed and that it represented the survival of an ancient pagan fertility religion. The two trials in question are those of the North Berwick witches, which took place in 1591, and that of Isabel Gowdie, which was held in 1662.

The existence of a group of witches which held meetings in North Berwick church was first suspected by a certain David Seaton who had become aware that one of his servants, Gilly Duncan, had acquired a local reputation as a healer. Interrogated by Seaton, who thought fit to use the 'pilliwinks' (thumbscrews) upon the girl, the maid confessed that all her cures were made with the aid of devils and that she herself was a witch. She also named various of her supposed associates, amongst them Agnes Sampson a midwife, Euphemia Maclean the daughter of a peer, and John Fian, the schoolmaster whose amorous involvement with a cow was described on page 52.

King James VI of Scotland, whose book on witchcraft was intended as a counter-blast against the scepticism of Reginald Scot, who personally interrogated some of the North Berwick witches.

High treason

When Fian and the other accused were first examined they protested their innocence but, after tortures of severity equal to those employed 30 years later in the *Hexenhaus* at Bamberg, they made not only the usual admissions but confessed to high treason. Under the command of their chief, the Devil, who had appeared in the form of a man clad in black gown and hat, they had attempted to murder King James VI of Scotland. They had attempted to sink a ship on which the King had been voyaging, they had employed image magic against him, and they had extracted a magic venom from the body of a black toad which they had intended to smear on a piece of the King's used clothing, thus poisoning him by sympathetic magic.

Fian later withdrew his confession and, in spite of further torture, remained steadfast in his denials of involvement in witchcraft until he was burned in Edinburgh. Agnes Sampson showed less fortitude, expanding her confession and telling how she and other witches had passed an image from hand to hand while saying 'This is King James VI, ordained to be consumed at the instance of a nobleman, Francis Earl Bothwell'.

This has led some to suggest that Francis Hepburn, Earl of Bothwell, was the leader of an organized witch cult, the survival of an ancient pagan faith, and that he was the 'Devil' of Agnes Sampson's confession who supposedly had presided over large gatherings of witches. One of them, according to the confession, had taken place in North Berwick church and had been attended by some 200 people.

However, this is unlikely. If one accepts that the Earl of Bothwell was the Devil who conducted the North Berwick meeting, and that the events described by Agnes Sampson actually took place, then one is also forced not only to accept that a great Scottish nobleman, a relation of King James VI, solemnly raised his gown and bent over so that 200 witches could kiss his behind, but that he had the power of flying over the sea.

Elf shot and fairies

Isabel Gowdie was tried as a witch as a consequence of her own confession, made quite voluntarily and without the imposition of torture. The wife of a farmer, she simply approached the Elders of the kirk and told them that since 1647, 15 years before, she had served the Devil.

The spontaneity of her confession has led some writers of witchcraft, such as the late Dr Margaret Murray, to regard it as a truthful account of the religious celebrations of an ancient cult. However, such writers have quoted very selectively from the confession, the full version of which contains so many fantastic elements that it is difficult to believe that it was the product of anything other than a schizophrenic illness.

Thus, she described how she and others had flown through the air and, making themselves as small as bees, had crawled through tiny holes in order to steal beer; how she had seen Satan manufacturing 'elf shot', flint arrow heads which witches were reputed to use for murderous purposes; and even how she had visited fairyland and talked to its King and Queen.

Isabel Gowdie's mental fantasies provide no better evidence for the existence of the witch cult than do confessions extracted by torture.

The witches of North Berwick were alleged to have danced widdershins, by which is meant counter-clockwise, around the Church in which the Devil had preached to them.

Hopkins' brutal methods of interrogation led many innocent victims of his activities to confess that they kept strangely-named 'familiar spirits' – demons who had assumed animal forms.

tions on a European scale are not to be found in the history of English witch trials.

Social outcasts

Very few victims of English witch hunts were men and women of social standing. Most of them seem to have been members of families of village outcasts whose quarrels with their neighbours had resulted in an

Matthew Hopkins, the self-appointed 'Witch Finder General' who at the time of the English Civil War was responsible for the executions of many supposed witches in the Puritan-dominated counties of East Anglia.

English witch hunts and persecutions were mild by the standards of those of Scotland or Continental Europe, and while suspected witches were brutally treated and cruelly interrogated they were not submitted to torture by the thumbscrew or the rack. Nor, contrary to popular belief, were English witches burned at the stake, this fate being reserved for heretics and traitors.

Rather surprisingly witchcraft as such was not a capital offence in England. Under the Witchcraft Act of 1563 the death penalty, carried out by hanging, was reserved for those found guilty of murder by sorcery; lesser bewitchments were punished by the pillory and imprisonment.

Probably as a consequence of the fact that English witchcraft suspects were questioned without being tortured, it was unusual for them to supply lists of names of those who had accompanied them to the Sabbath. The snowball effect, the initiation and growth of a persecution powered by a cycle of arrest-confession-denunciation-more arrests, was thus largely absent from English witch hunts and reports of mass execu-

In 1643 Puritan witch beliefs led a Parliamentary soldier to shoot dead a supposed witch who was, in fact, an innocent woman using large wooden pattens to walk on the mud-flats of the River Kennett.

exceptional unpopularity. This was certainly true of, for example, the St Osyth witches of 1582 and the Lancashire witches of 1611.

The nearest equivalent to a mass persecution on a scale approaching continental models would seem to have taken place in East Anglia during the period 1644–6, a time when the war between King and Parliament had led to a partial breakdown of law and order and an increase in social tensions. The main instigator of this persecution was Matthew Hopkins, a lawyer turned witch hunter who in 1644 commenced his unpleasant career at Manningtree in Essex when he discovered, so he said, the existence of a group of local witches. He managed to get 29 of these condemned, four of them being hanged for attempting to murder Hopkins by sending a demon to attack him in his garden.

Inspired by this success, he started to call himself Witch Finder General and induced various towns in East Anglia to employ him and two assistants to search out supposed witches. In his first year of witch hunting he seems to have been responsible for over 60 deaths, and over a period of three years his victims may have totalled over 200.

The biter bit

To induce confessions Hopkins employed torments which, while they did not involve the shedding of blood or the breaking of bones, admirably served his purpose. Such torments were typified by those inflicted by Hopkins and his gang on John Lowe, the elderly vicar of the Suffolk parish of Brandeston, who was kept awake for night after night and forced to walk until his feet were blistered. Eventually he confessed to witchcraft — he had sent an imp, he said, to sink a ship — and was hanged at Framlingham.

Hopkins' persecutions were confined to strongly Puritan areas of East Anglia and it seems probable that most of his victims were known to be anti-Puritan — certainly John Lowe seems to have died a faithful member of the Church of England. Curiously enough, however, the man responsible for the downfall of Hopkins, a minister named John Gaule, was himself a Puritan. In 1646, Gaule published a pamphlet which hinted that Hopkins was himself a witch. The suggestion was taken up by others and, in May 1647, Hopkins was hanged for the offence for which he had sent so many to their deaths.

In August 1986, Mr and Mrs Smurl of West Pittston, Pennsylvania, gave a press conference at which they claimed that for the previous 18 months they had shared their home with what they described as 'a demonic horde'. Dark, vaguely human forms with grossly distorted heads had been seen, monstrous swine-like snortings had been heard, and the Smurl home had been filled with a sulphurous stench 'so thick it was almost suffocating'. Even the family dog, a German Shepherd, had been subjected to diabolical attack, being slammed against the walls by unseen hands.

There was nothing new in the nature of the demonic attacks to which the Smurl family supposedly was subjected, and similar uncanny happenings have been reported since the earliest period of European settlement in North America. In 17th-century New England they were regarded as almost commonplace and usually attributed to the activities of witches.

Foreordained to salvation

Witchcraft was a near obsession with some of the Puritan ministers of the Commonwealth of Massachu-

Most of the inhabitants of the Massachusetts of 1692 believed in the reality of the Witches' Sabbath as deeply as their ancestors had done two centuries earlier.

setts and the other New England colonies and, remarkably, this can be at least partly attributed to the fact that a young Englishman, a student at Cambridge, got very drunk in the autumn of 1578.

William Perkins, the student in question, had stumbled out of an alehouse and begun to stagger towards his lodgings when he passed a young mother carrying a screaming infant. 'Hush', she threatened the child, 'or drunken Perkins will get you'.

Men and women of the 16th century sometimes interpreted quite ordinary happenings as conveying messages from God, and the presentation of himself as a nursery bogeyman was understood by Perkins as a divine command to repent of his sins. He became sober, ceased blaspheming, devoted himself to study and prayer, and became convinced that he was one of the Elect, a soul whom God had foreordained to salvation. Within a dozen or so years Perkins became the world's leading exponent of the harsh theology of Calvinism, his writings studied as far away as Poland and Hungary, and regarded as only second in authority to those of John Calvin himself.

This sign, on display near 20th-century Salem, was put up by John Beresford Hatch, a man who had a burning desire to defend the reputations of those hanged for witchcraft in 1692.

Nowhere were Perkins' books esteemed more than in 17th-century New England, the colonists being particularly impressed by his treatise, *A Discourse of the Damned Art of Witchcraft*.

The Church of hell

Perkins's *Discourse*, written as a counterblast to the scepticism of Reginald Scot (*see* page 76), denounced exorcism as a superstitious practice for which prayer and fasting should be substituted. Save for this, however, the beliefs of its Calvinist author were similar to those of Catholic demonologists of the same period.

Like them Perkins uncritically accepted accounts of supernormal phenomena supposedly associated with witchcraft. Like them he believed that witches were members of an organized conspiracy, a sort of 'Church of Hell' directed by Satan himself. Like them he believed that the 'white witch' who blessed rather than cursed was as guilty as the 'black witch'.

Perkins's beliefs seem to have been totally and unconditionally accepted by the leaders of the New England settlers and the first North American witch trial of which records survive took place as early as 1647. Over the next 40 years or so there were at least 80 other New England witch trials and at least 22 convicted witches were hanged. Thus, for example, 'Goody' Glover was executed at Boston in 1688 for bewitching the children of John Goodwin. In the following year a young minister included a lengthy account of the bewitchment of the Goodwin children in a book entitled *Memorable Providences*. That minister was Cotton Mather, a man who was to play a sinister part in the persecution of the Salem witches of 1692.

The English-speaking settlers of North America took the witchcraft beliefs of the Old World to the New and would tell their children the stories of such notorious English witches as Elizabeth Sawyer, executed in 1621.

Cotton Mather, born in 1663, was a man of many curious beliefs. Most of them were probably harmless enough, but one of them sent innocent men and women to the gallows. This was his assertion, derived from the theologian William Perkins, that an unsupported 'Confession after due Examination' was adequate evidence on which to find guilty those accused of witchcraft. As Mather wrote:

> *Among the sufficient means of Conviction, the first is the free and voluntary Confession of the Crime, made by the party suspected and accused, after Examination . . . taken upon pregnant assumption. What needs now more witness or further Enquiry?*

Throughout the course of the New England witch trials of 1692 this belief, that voluntary confession was sufficient evidence for conviction, dominated the proceedings of the courts. 'Voluntary' confessions, which in this context were statements extracted by bullying examiners from exhausted prisoners deprived of sleep, food and drink, sent many to their deaths.

Odd postures and antick gestures

The Salem witch craze began when, early in 1692, Elizabeth Parris, nine-year-old daughter of the minister of Salem Village, and her eleven-year-old cousin, Abigail Williams, began to adopt what one observer called 'odd postures and antick gestures'. In other words they began to exhibit the symptoms of bewitchment. They:

> *. . . were bitten and pinched by invisible agents . . . Sometimes they were taken dumb, their mouths stopped, their throats stopped, their limbs wracked and tormented so as might move an heart of stone . . .*

George Jacobus, one of those accused of witchcraft at Salem, was hanged in August 1692. Subsequently all his property was confiscated, even his wife's wedding ring being seized.

Spectral evidence

The bewitched children were soon denouncing as witches men and women who had previously been regarded as being of the utmost respectability. They included Martha Corey and Rebecca Nurse, both Church members in good standing, and a Congregational minister, George Burroughs. The first six hangings took place in July. One of those hanged, Rebecca Nurse, had actually been found not guilty by a jury but was still executed.

Hysterical credulity, deliberately sustained and encouraged by Cotton Mather and others, became general and great weight was given to 'spectral evidence' – supernatural experiences which witnesses claimed to have undergone. One witness, for example, claimed that the spirit of the dead wife of one accused man had appeared to her and told her that she had been murdered by her husband.

By October 1692 such evidence had resulted in over 20 executions and something like 200 arrests. Accusations had been made by the supposedly bewitched girls against yet another 200 people, including the President of Harvard and the wife of the Governor of Massachusetts. Quite suddenly public opinion changed. Those under arrest were pardoned and released, those who had been hanged were posthumously rehabilitated. The Salem witch mania was over.

Cotton Mather's somewhat philosophical features masked a profound credulity – he seriously claimed that part of the Salem Meeting House had been torn down by 'a Daemon Invisibly Entring'.

The girls' behaviour proved infectious and by the middle of March about ten people, including four married women and 'an ancient woman named Goodall', were exhibiting all the signs of demonic attack.

By this time some of those afflicted had made specific accusations against people whom they named as witches. They said that Tituba, an Indian woman who was a slave in Mr Parris' household, 'did pinch, prick and grievously torment them' although she was not visibly present. Named as witches at the same time were Sarah Good, who may have been of unsound mind, and Sarah Osburn, an elderly invalid who seems to have been generally unpopular with the village of Salem, because she had once lived with a man to whom she was not married.

Tituba and the two Sarahs were arrested and examined. The former, as a result of beatings and threats, made a full confession of the type familiarly encountered in European witch trials. She and the other two accused had met Satan, had signed agreements with him, had bewitched the afflicted girls and had flown through the air. As Mr Roger Thompson pointed out in his *The Witches of Salem*, Tituba's confession dragged Salem Village into the world of *Malleus Maleficarum* in which almost anybody, not just village scapegoats such as the two Sarahs, could be suspected of witchcraft.

In the book of which the title page is reproduced here, Mather asserted that the 'Rampant Hag Martha Carrier' had been chosen by Satan to be Queen of Hell. Martha was executed on 19 August 1692.

The Wonders of the Invisible World :

Being an Account of the

T R Y A L S

OF

Several Witches,

Lately Executed in

NEW-ENGLAND:

And of several remarkable.Curiosities therein Occurring.

Together with,

I. Observations upon the Nature, the Number, and the Operations of the Devils.

II. A short Narrative of a late outrage committed by a knot of Witches in Swede-Land, very much resembling, and so far explaining, that under which New-England has laboured.

III. Some Councels directing a due Improvement of the Terrible things lately done by the unusual and amazing Range of Evil-Spirits in New-England.

IV. A brief Discourse upon those Temptations which are the more ordinary Devices of Satan.

By *COTTON MATHER.*

The Catholic Church always has taught that the Christian soul is subject to the help of angels and the wiles of demons. Sister Maria Renata was believed to have been an accomplice of the latter.

The events which took place at Salem in 1692 marked the end of the great witch hunts, for a conviction of the reality of witchcraft and demonic possession was in rapid decline amongst educated Christians. Belief had been almost universal in 1600, had become very much a subject of sceptical debate by 1700 and was rare amongst literate people by the beginning of the 19th century.

The decline in belief was a slow process, and even in the middle of the 18th century a substantial number of Christians, both Catholic and Protestant, felt that to disbelieve totally in the existence of witchcraft and possession was to reject the teachings of scripture. Had not, they asked, Saul, Israel's first king, consulted the witch of Endor? And had not Jesus dismissed a horde of demons from their human victim and compelled them to enter the Gadarene swine? The attitude of such people was well expressed by John Wesley, founder of the Methodist Church, who affirmed that to deny the existence of witches and demons was incompatible with a belief in the inspiration of the Bible.

Broomsticks

Not only did witch beliefs linger on, even amongst the literate, until well into the 18th century, but isolated trials of supposed witches continued until a surprisingly late date. Perhaps the most spectacular of these late trials was that of a German nun, Sister Maria Renata Sanger von Mossau, which took place at Wurzburg in 1749. The nature of these made it apparent that the most extravagant assertions of the demonologists of the 15th and 16th centuries were still given credence by some – that, for example, witches flew on broomsticks.

Sister Maria Renata, born in 1679, had entered the convent at Unterzell in 1698 and lived a quiet religious

Roasting alive was a traditional punishment for German witches. In view of her age, Sister Maria Renata's judges allowed her to be beheaded before being burned.

An unclean demon of the night about to embrace a sleeping woman is shown in this painting by Henry Fuseli. The willing acceptance of such embraces was one of the supposed crimes of Sister Maria Renata.

life until 1744, in which year she became sub-prioress. In the following year a certain Sister Cecilia, the daughter of an Italian mercantile family which was resident in Hamburg, was admitted as a novice and almost immediately began to exhibit the classic symptoms of supposed demonic possession. That is to say, she went into violent contortions, spoke in a strange voice and purported to see visions of hell and its inhabitants. Such behaviour proved as contagious as the similar antics which had disturbed convents a century and more before, and within a short time five others were exhibiting symptoms of possession and bewitchment.

Yellow robe of Satan

Sister Maria Renata looked upon the behaviour of the afflicted nuns as symptomatic of hysteria, not possession – a dangerous opinion, for it aroused suspicion that she herself was in some way anxious to hide the 'fact' that Satan was at work in the convent.

Suspicion increased when an elderly nun on her deathbed told both the Prioress and her confessor that she was dying as a result of Sister Maria Renata's bewitchments. Such an accusation could not be disregarded and it was reported to the Bishop of Wurzburg, who ordered that the accused sub-prioress should be arrested and her cell searched.

The search disclosed some ointments, some dried herbs and a yellow robe. Under torture Sister Maria Renata confessed that the herbs and ointments were poisons, that clad in the yellow robe she had flown on a broomstick to the Sabbath and that she had copulated with demons since she was eight years old. In view of the fact that Sister Maria Renata was in her seventieth year the Bishop of Wurzburg decided to be merciful – that is, he ordered her to be beheaded before her body was burned at the stake. As the flames consumed the body a Jesuit, Father Gaar, preached an edifying sermon to those who looked on.

HINDERING WITCHES FROM THEIR WILL

With the general cessation of official legal intervention in cases of supposed witchcraft and sorcery those who believe that they were victims of the evil eye, ill wishing and black magic were forced to use traditional folk magic for their own protection.

Quite a number of herbs were employed for such purposes and according to a widespread folk belief:

Rue, Vervain and Dill
Hinder Witches from their Will.

Even more effective against witchcraft, so it was believed by farmers and peasants throughout northern Europe, were the leaves, fruit and wood of the rowan, or mountain ash. To prevent horses being ridden by the hags of the night, or cows from having their udders sucked dry by witches' imps, a peasant would tie a rowan twig to the animals' halters or place rowan

This attractive bottle, now in the City of London's Guildhall Museum, had been used for magical purposes. When it was discovered at St Paul's Pier wharf, it contained a cloth heart stuck with pins.

Those who defended themselves against witchcraft believed that sorcerers used such objects as heads torn from living cats, skulls and dead bats in the course of their sinister proceedings.

branches in the stable and cowshed. Sometimes, as an additional protection, milking stools and pails were made of rowan wood and in many parts of Europe crossed rowan twigs were employed for the same purpose. As late as the middle of the last century, it was recorded that in parts of eastern England rowan twig crosses were to be seen over the entrances of almost every cottage, stable, cowshed and pigsty.

Normally these crosses were renewed each May Day – in some places called Rowan Tree Day – and it was believed that they were particularly potent if the twigs from which they were made came from a tree which the harvester had never seen until he cropped its branches.

The unquiet dead

A rowan cross was sometimes placed above a child's cradle in order to protect it from bewitchment or from being stolen by fairies, the mysterious and often sinister allies of witchcraft; and in parts of both Wales and England it was at one time customary to plant rowan in churchyards in order to prevent the unquiet dead from leaving their graves and disturbing the peace of the living. In the 17th century, John Evelyn noted that 'there is not a churchyard without one of them planted in it' and that on 'a certain day' the common people wore rowan crosses.

Rowan berries, bright red in colour, were also believed to be protective against witchcraft and disease and were sometimes strung together and hung like a necklace around the neck of the supposed victim of sorcery.

Those wealthy enough to be able to afford a necklace more durable than red berries employed one made of red coral for the same protective purpose. This custom was referred to by Reginald Scot in his *Discoverie of Witchcraft*: 'the coral preserveth such as bear it from fascination or bewitching . . . they are hanged about children's necks'.

Witch bottles

Anything red seems to have been considered a possible defence against witchcraft. Probably this is because red is the colour of blood, and thus of life, while witchcraft was looked upon as essentially barren and anti-life. Certainly blood was an important ingredient of the 'witch bottle', a white magic potion intended to go on the offensive against witchcraft rather than protect from it.

A witch bottle was sometimes made of glass and sometimes of metal. In it were placed blood and urine from a bewitched person together with some of the victim's hair and nail clippings. It was set beside a cottage fire and slowly heated while all present said the Lord's Prayer over and over again. As the bottle heated so would the guilty witch or sorcerer feel increasing discomfort and be drawn towards the witch bottle. The first person to arrive would be 'scored above the breath', scratched on the forehead, which would break the spell and restore its victim to normality.

When witch bottles, used in defensive magical spells, were heated before a fire they often burst. Cunning Murrell, an Essex white witch who flourished in the 1860s, had his forged from iron.

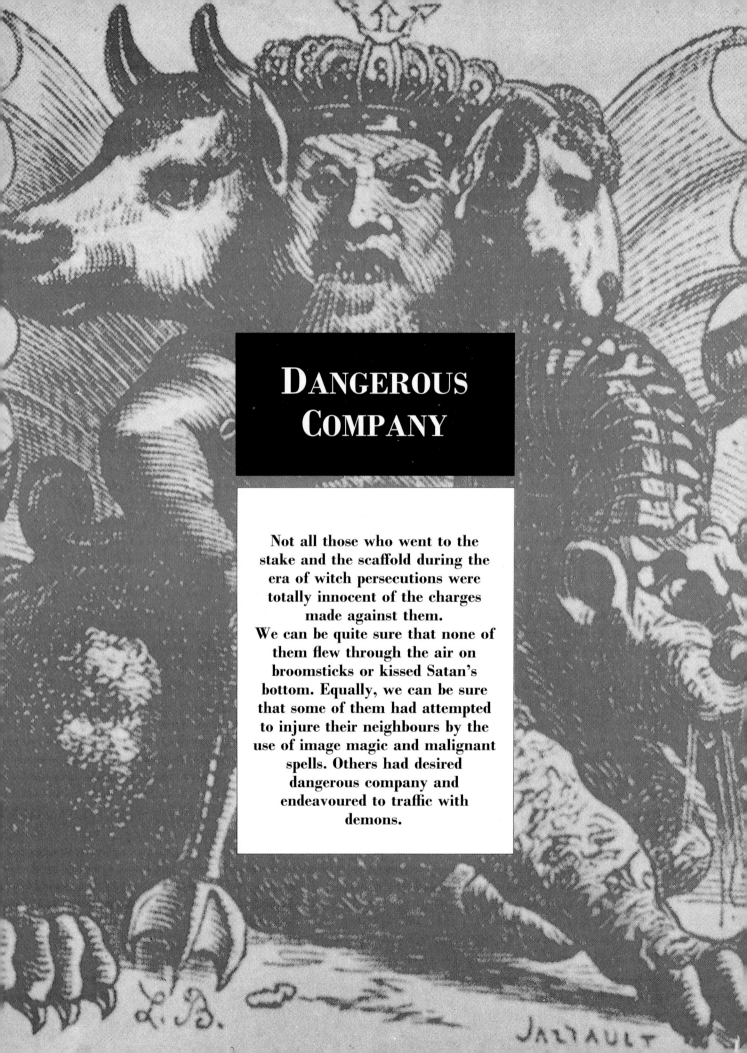

DANGEROUS COMPANY

Not all those who went to the stake and the scaffold during the era of witch persecutions were totally innocent of the charges made against them.

We can be quite sure that none of them flew through the air on broomsticks or kissed Satan's bottom. Equally, we can be sure that some of them had attempted to injure their neighbours by the use of image magic and malignant spells. Others had desired dangerous company and endeavoured to traffic with demons.

SOLOMON AND THE DEVILS

It was believed in the Middle Ages that the demon Belial, one of the princes of hell, and his subordinates paid formal homage to King Solomon.

In the oases of the Sahara, professional story tellers are still to be found plying their ancient trade. They sit upon the ground, surrounded by an attentive audience, and recount tales both new and old. Amongst the most popular of the latter are those which deal with 'Suleiman ben-Daoud' – Solomon, son of David – and his dealings with angels and demons.

The historical Solomon was the 10th-century King of Israel who, as is told in the Old Testament, built the first Temple in Jerusalem, sent great trading fleets to the ports of the Mediterranean, and was so renowned for his power and his wisdom that the great Queen of the Arabian state of Sheba undertook the long journey to Jerusalem so that she might learn from him.

Solomon was the last King of a united Israel. After him the state became divided, subject to civil strife and foreign invasions, and the history of the Solomonic period began to acquire legendary accretions. It was thought of as a golden age, in which the rulers of the earth had paid homage to Israel's King, a being possessed of superhuman powers.

The ring and the rocks

One of the things which most impressed Jews of the centuries subsequent to the reign of King Solomon was that the huge Temple he had ordered to be raised took only seven years to build. Surely, it was said, ordinary human beings could not have been capable of this feat; Solomon's builders must have been the recipients of supernatural aid from angels or demons.

Typical of the legends which grew up about Solomon was that concerning the shaped stones of which the Temple was built. To split rocks into stones of the desired size was no easy task for Solomon's workmen for, according to legend, God had forbidden that any tools made of iron should be used in the construction of the Temple. What was needed was a knowledge of the way to control the 'shamir', a huge worm believed to have the ability to split and shape stone.

Solomon knew that the demon Asmodeus was possessed of this knowledge so he sent a warrior named Benaiah to capture the demon and make him a slave. Benaiah, realizing that his weapons of war would be powerless against Asmodeus, tricked the demon into getting drunk and then, by the use of a magic ring engraved with the secret name of God, reduced the Prince of Hell to servitude.

King Asmodeus

Asmodeus at first obeyed all of Solomon's commands. He taught the King how to obtain the 'shamir' from its rightful owner, the angel of the sea, and how to control it; he laboured long and hard on the building of the Temple; and in time taught the King all the secrets of magic.

Eventually, however, after the Temple had been completed, Asmodeus managed to get hold of the magic ring which had reduced him to slavery. Using its powers he overcame Solomon's magic, expelled the King from Jerusalem and, assuming the form of the monarch, ruled Israel in his stead until Solomon regained his ring three years later.

A ring which enabled its user to control demons was clearly a desirable object. Soon there came into existence some books, attributed to Solomon, which taught how it could be made.

A French edition of the *Key of Solomon*, a magical textbook which probably derives from a lost Greek original but which some still believe to have been compiled by Solomon himself.

'The ring of Solomon', says a 16th-century textbook of ritual magic, 'preserves the magus from the stinking sulphurous breath of evil spirits'. The authorship of many of such instructional magical texts, which were circulated in manuscript during the Middle Ages and the Renaissance, was attributed to Solomon, the best known of them being the *Clavicula Salomonis*, that is 'the little key of Solomon'.

As early as the first century AD, the Jewish historian Josephus mentioned a magical book, supposedly written by Solomon, which was in the possession of an exorcist named Eleazar, and a Greek manuscript

entitled *The Testament of Solomon* dates from only two centuries or so later. The earliest version of this which survives is largely a list of demons and the 'names of power' which supposedly enable the magician to control them. The names and mystic words given seem to have been derived from not only Jewish, but also Christian, Persian and Egyptian sources.

Names of power

Curiously enough the *Clavicula Salomonis* bears very little resemblance to the Testament of Solomon, so almost certainly the many manuscript versions of the former derive from a quite different and lost original – perhaps from a book mentioned by Psellus, an 11th-century Greek author, which he attributed to Solomon and described as dealing with both the evocation of demons and the mystic qualities of engraved gemstones. Certainly Greek manuscripts of the *Clavicula* were in circulation by the 14th century and it was probably a Latin or French translation of this which was the *Book of Solomon*. In the middle of the 14th century, Pope Innocent VI ordered this book to be destroyed on

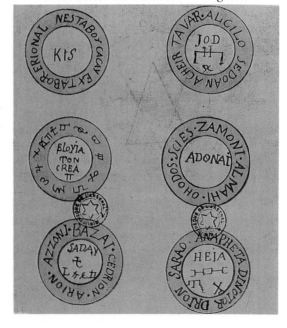

Pentacles – magical symbols – which according to the compiler of this *grimoire* would obtain the help of 'good spirits'. The Church taught that these beliefs were demons in disguise.

The demon Mammon, one of the four great princes of hell, as represented in a 16th-century *grimoire* – a text describing how to evoke devils.

the grounds that it advocated 'sacrifices to demons'.

There is no reason to doubt that, in truth, such sacrifices were offered by ritual magicians of the later Middle Ages and the Renaissance. With one or two exceptions, all surviving textbooks of ritual magic from the period in question include processes involving either blood sacrifice or the use of potions in which the blood of animals or birds is an ingredient.

The *Clavicula* and other books of a similar nature were referred to as *grimoires*, i.e., 'grammars'. No doubt this was because the correct use of 'words and names of power' has always been the central core of ceremonial magic.

Solomon's garters

Most of the processes outlined in the *grimoires* show a certain ambivalence. On the one hand the magician is instructed to recite lengthy and piously expressed prayers to God and his angels. On the other, these same prayers are intended to produce effects which are at best silly expressions of petty malevolence or greed – the prevention of a hunter from killing any game, for example, or the ability to cheat at games of dice without being detected. At their worst the results which the magician supposedly can obtain by his use of prayer, incense and incantation are unpleasant and wicked – he can hold conversations with demons, take on the appearance of a woman's husband in order to trick himself into that woman's bed, and murder his enemies by magic.

On the whole, it is not surprising that the Church condemned the use of *grimoires*, considering them the literature of hell and regarding all who employed the techniques they taught as engaging in devil worship.

Yet, there is no doubt at all that at least some students of the *grimoires* were priests, men who found it compatible with their vocation to spend time in such unlikely occupations as manufacturing 'the garters of Solomon' (which were believed to confer the power of flight), finding buried treasure, and attempting to become invisible.

DANGEROUS EVEN TO THINK UPON

Most works describing the techniques of ritual magic and demon evocation, from late Egyptian papyri to Renaissance *grimoires*, are replete with 'words and names of power' which were believed to enable the evoker to control demons and spirits. Such words and names were described in classical times as 'barbarous words of evocation', for they seemed to be in no known language but to consist of no more than long strings of meaningless syllables. In reality, such words were often corrupted forms of the names of the gods of Assyria, Egypt and Babylon.

In even more corrupt form some of these names, passed down through generations of magicians and sorcerers, survived into the 16th and 17th centuries and are to be found in magical works of that period. From about 1500, however, most of the 'words of power' given in *grimoires* are of Hebrew origin and derive from the Jewish esoteric system known as the 'kabalah'.

Secret traditions

According to Jewish legend, the kabalah was a secret tradition concerning the rightful interpretation of scripture which had been given to mankind by the archangel Metratron. In reality it was a mystical system, evolved in the Middle Ages and the Renaissance, in which great importance was attached to the names of God, his archangels and his angels. It was these divine and angelic names, often in an almost unrecognizably corrupt form, which were incorporated into many of the spells given in the *grimoires* and were supposed to enable the magician to control the demons he had evoked.

The kabalists themselves were almost as concerned with demons as were sorcerers and magicians and they evolved a complex demonology which exerted a strong influence on Western magic and still has its devotees.

The sephiroth or divine emanations were believed by cabbalists to have evil and averse aspects – the Kingdom of the Shells – where unbalanced force reigned and demons dwelt.

Most students and practitioners of the type of ritual magic taught in the *grimoires* have not gone so far as to identify Satan and Jehovah. Nevertheless, some of them have exhibited a desire for an acquaintance with the demons of kabalistic and other Jewish legend. This seems unhealthy in view of the fact that one kabalistic text warns that these demons are 'dangerous even to think upon'.

One such demon, Lilith, seems to have appealed particularly to magicians past and present. According to legend Lilith was the first wife of Adam, made from filth before the creation of Eve. She left her husband because she objected to him lying on top of her during sexual intercourse – she felt herself his equal and that copulation should take place lying side by side – and went off to mate with fallen angels who spawned a great family of demons upon her. These are the *lilim*, exact equivalents of the *succubi* of the Christian demonologists, who seduce and weaken men in the silence of the night.

A 19th-century portrait of Hakeldama, an unpleasant demon believed in by some cabbalistic magicians, whose name was probably derived from that of the place where the body of Judas Iscariot was buried.

The demonic forces of the kabalists were described as the 'klippoth', or 'shells', and were seen by the great kabalistic mystics as having their roots in the divine mystery – the idea being that in itself evil is no more than the dead residue of the life of the spirit, and that it only manifests itself in demonic form when it is nourished by human sin which, paradoxically, has always within it an element of the divine.

Order and wisdom

The very complex ideas of the kabalists concerning the origin of evil were perverted by some practitioners of demonic magic into a simple belief that 'God' and 'Satan' were just different names for the same being. One magician who adopted this curious and dangerous theory said that:

Jehovah is but a synonym of Satan, sometimes called the Prince of Light and sometimes the Prince of Darkness. This is the awful secret of the Qabalah [sic] . . . to the unpurified and the uninitiated its knowledge means anarchy and death, yet to us order and wisdom.

Lilith, demon queen of cabbalistic myth and legend, traditionally was believed to have procreated a horde of unclean female spirits who engaged in sexual relationships with sleeping men.

According to the late Montague Summers, an authority on witchcraft and black magic, this portrait of Cassiel, the spirit of Saturn, was 'painted from life' by his evoker.

'A stunted dwarf with large head and ears ... lips green and slobbery'. This description of the demon Nimorup, one of the forty-nine servants of that Prince of Hell named Beelzebub – which means 'Lord of the Flies' – was given by a 20th-century psychic, daughter of an English clergyman, who claimed to have seen this unpleasant entity. Her detailed descriptions of Nimorup's fellows were equally alarming and few of us would care to encounter such creatures as Nominon, for example, whom the same psychic saw as a gigantic 'red spongy jellyfish with one luminous spot, like a nasty mess'.

Oriax and Agares

Older descriptions of demons as they were believed to manifest themselves to ritual magicians seem equally unappealing. Thus, for example, a 16th-century version of a *grimoire* ascribed to Solomon, the *Lemegeton*, says that a demon named Oriax appears: '. . . with the face of a lion, riding upon a horse mighty and strong, with a serpent's tail; and he holdeth in his right hand two great serpents hissing'. As one 20th-century magician pointed out, it is unclear from this description whether it is Oriax or his steed which has a serpent's tail. In either case his visible form would seem to be somewhat offputting, as would that of Agares, a demon described as 'mild in appearance' although he manifests himself 'riding upon a crocodile and carrying a goshawk upon his fist'.

Portraits of some of the Princes of Hell were included in *The Magus* (1801), a curious collection of *grimoires* and other occult texts which was compiled by Francis Barrett, an alcoholic apothecary and balloonist who also dabbled in alchemy, magic and other strange arts. Some of the beings portrayed look harmless enough – Apollyon, for example, resembles an old clothes dealer from whose shoulders wings have sprouted, a form which is at variance with his reputation as 'Lord of the demons of discords, war and devastation'.

Others are shown in more traditional form and Cassiel's portrait as 'a bearded ancient king riding upon a dragon' is particularly sinister, the more so in view of an occult tradition, recorded by the late Montague Summers, that it was drawn from life. At one time or another Barrett is reputed to have evoked most of the princes of the infernal regions to visible appearance.

An early 19th-century periodical publication, the strangely named *Straggling Astrologer*, featured this picture of the demons which its editor believed that he could summon from hell.

The mysterious symbols and letters at the foot of this document have been claimed to have been written by devils, signing their agreement to a pact with a sorcerer.

The power of names

Many *grimoires* consist of little more than long lists of the names of demons and angels together with their 'seals'. By seals were meant abstract designs of varying complexity, each one of which was associated with a particular spirit, good or bad.

The importance attached to the names of demons and other spirits derived from the ancient belief that to know the true name of another living creature gave one power over it. In some primitive cultures it was customary for the real name of a child to be kept secret from everyone save its parents lest some sorcerer, witch or evil spirit should learn it and thus gain power over that child.

The seal of a demon was considered to be a diagrammatic representation of the real name of that same demon. By subjecting to occult manipulations a piece of vellum on which a particular seal had been drawn or a metal talisman on which it had been engraved, a magician could, so it was believed, induce the appropriate demon to obey his will. What particular seal was chosen by the magician for his working would depend upon the nature of the magician's desires. Thus, the seal of Stolas would be used for the purpose of knowing the 'virtues of herbs', that of Vovall to 'procure the love of women', and that of Kimaris to discover hidden treasure.

*Was this the face that launched a thousand ships
And burnt the topless towers of Ilium?*

So, in the play written by the Elizabethan dramatist Christopher Marlowe, spoke the magician Faustus when he beheld the features of Helen of Troy, whose phantom he had summoned from the underworld.

Marlowe took most of the incidents of his play, including that of the evocation of the shade of Helen, from the *Faustbuch*, published at Frankfurt in 1587, which told how a theologian named Dr Johannes Faustus had obtained a magical book, a *grimoire*, and with its help had summoned a demon from hell and sold his soul to the Devil. The *Faustbuch* ended on a high moral note with the magician being carried off to Hell by the devils with whom he had held commerce. It was this which seems to have endeared the *Faustbuch* to theologians and preachers, who accepted it as a truthful and awful warning of the dangers of dabbling in sorcery.

Cannibalism

Stories concerning Faust, his strange powers and his dramatic end, date from long before the *Faustbuch*. Martin Luther referred to such tales in his table talk, clearly regarding them as veracious, while Melanchthon, Luther's friend and fellow reformer, casually mentioned Faust as having eaten a rival magician and having possessed the power of flight.

Then great Agrippa foams with rage—
Look at him on this very page!
He seizes Arthur, seizes Ned,
Takes William by his little head;

And they may scream and kick and call,
Into the ink he dips them all;
Into the inkstand, one, two, three,
Till they are black as black can be:
Turn over now, and you shall see.

In time the legends concerning Faustus became attached to Cornelius Agrippa, perhaps the greatest of 16th-century occult philosophers, who thus became a bogey to frighten naughty children.

The title page of this racy English translation of the 16th-century German *Faustbuch* shows the magician clad in the robes of a Doctor of Laws and standing within a protective magical circle.

Some preachers claimed to have encountered Faust in person and to have witnessed his magical feats. Thus, as early as 1548, Johann Gast, a Swiss Protestant, claimed that he had once had dinner with the magician at Basle. Not only had the meal consisted of out-of-season food – clear evidence of diabolical intervention – but the servant who dished it up had been a demon in disguise. This demon, said Gast, usually took the form of a dog which accompanied Faust on his walks. Faust's horse, he added, was also a demon.

In spite of the ludicrous nature of such claims, there is not doubt that Faust was an historical character – or, perhaps, two or three historical characters. For there are references to both a Georgius and Johann Faust, both magicians, and it seems likely that one or both of these was imitating an original Faust, also a sorcerer.

In a letter of August 1507, the Abbot Trithemius of Spanheim warned his correspondent against a man 'who is a fool and no philosopher', who was calling himself 'Faustus *Junior*, Fountain of Necromancers, astrologer, magus secundus . . .' From this it can be assumed that there was once a now forgotten 'Faustus Senior' who was a master of necromancy, the raising of the spirits of the dead, and other black arts.

Dastardly lewdness

For a time the man about whom Trithemius had written so contemptuously earned his living as a schoolmaster at Kreuznach, but this ended when he fled the town after he had been accused of 'dastardly lewdness' with the boys he taught. He was almost certainly identical with the Georgius Faust of Helmstedt, who was

recorded as making wild occult prophecies in 1528.

Was he also, one wonders, the 'great sodomite and necromancer' Dr Faustus, who was refused a passport by the city of Nuremberg in 1532? Or was that the Johann Faust who received a theology degree at Heidelberg in 1509? And which Faust was it who was recorded as having studied magic at Cracow, practised it throughout Germany and, according to the writer Johannes Wier, claimed to be Satan's brother-in-law?

Authentic references to both Johann and Georgius are lacking after about 1540. Presumably one, or both, came to such an unpleasant end that they inspired the legend that grew up about him – or them.

The character of the original, and rather sordid, 16th-century Faustus – sodomite and sorcerer – was transmuted by the genius of Goethe into that of the rebel against God who eventually achieves redemption.

At the present day some practitioners of ritual magic still endeavour to apply the techniques taught in the *Clavicula Salomonis* and other occult textbooks of the type known as *grimoires*.

Manuscripts of such works are extremely rare, but printed versions of most of the best known *grimoires* are fairly easily available, although they are not always complete. Thus, the only available English language version of the *Clavicula Salomonis* in printed form is heavily expurgated, its editor and translator, MacGregor Mathers (1854–1918), having deleted most of the material which he considered to smack of black

Cornelius Agrippa, the supposed author of the *Fourth Book of Occult Philosophy*, the textbook of ritual magic which Thomas Parkes of Bristol used for the evocation of the spirits who supposedly destroyed him.

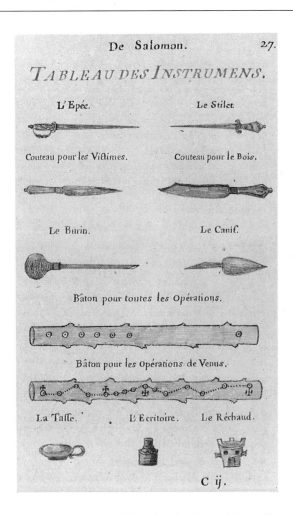

De Salomon. 27.

TABLEAU DES INSTRUMENS.

L'Epée.   Le Stilet.

Couteau pour les Victimes.   Couteau pour le Bois.

Le Burin.   Le Canif.

Bâton pour toutes les Opérations.

Bâton pour les Opérations de Venus.

La Tasse.   L'Ecritoire.   Le Réchaud.

C ij.

The apparatus used by the ritual magician, all of which had to be of his own making, was considerable. Just a few of the 'magical weapons' used, which included two types of wand, are shown here.

magic and demon worship.

Mathers was also the translator of a *grimoire* with the rather forbidding title of *The Sacred Magic of Abramelin the Mage*, a work which enjoys a high reputation amongst contemporary students of ceremonial magic, who regard it as standing in a class of its own.

Diabolical science

The author of *The Sacred Magic* seems to have disapproved of all *grimoires* save his own; they led one, he said, into making pacts with the Devil. He had himself known, so he said, a magician who had followed this course, a certain Antony of Prague who had:

> ... *made a pact with the Demon; and had given himself over to him in body and in soul ... the deceitful Leviathan had promised him forty years of life to do his pleasure ... He rendered himself invisible, he used to fly in the air, he used to enter through the keyholes into locked-up rooms ... Ultimately his body was found dragged through the streets, and his head without any tongue therein, lying in a drain. And this was all the profit he drew from his Diabolical Science and Magic.*

Whether or not Antony of Prague ever existed, and if he did whether he was destroyed by demons he had evoked, is problematical. There is little doubt, however, that some of those who experimented with the demonic magic of the *grimoires* had cause to regret it. They may not have been physically carried away by devils, but they were certainly destroyed by the interior, psychological 'demons' which had erupted into consciousness as a result of occult experimentation.

There is good reason to think that there have been victims of such unwise dabbling in the magic of the *grimoires* in our own century. Thus, for example, a well-known musician of the 1930s had a magical seal tattooed upon his skin with the intention of bringing about a certain desired event. He 'energised' the seal – kept his mind concentrated on that which it represented – by blistering his tattooed skin with a glowing cigarette. The desired event came about; shortly afterwards the musician committed suicide.

Faster than he wished

Sometimes actual delusions, somewhat similar to those experienced in delirium tremens, seem to have resulted from the use of the demonic magic of the *grimoires*. Typical of such victims of demons, exterior or interior, was Thomas Parkes, a young man living near Bristol towards the end of the 17th century.

According to both Protestant and Catholic theologians, the 'good spirits' with whom magicians claimed to be in contact were, in reality, devils expelled from heaven along with Lucifer.

Parkes was a clever young man of humble origins whose knowledge of mathematics and land surveying was sufficient to attract the admiration of his fellows. From the study of mathematics he went on to astrology – a fairly natural progression at that period – and from astrology to ceremonial magic.

Parkes' first experiment in *grimoire* magic resulted in the visible appearance of spirits 'in the shape of little girls, about a foot and a half high'. A later experiment ended disastrously. Spirits, recorded a local clergyman, appeared to Parkes 'faster than he wished them' in the shape of lions, bears and serpents. He found it beyond his powers to banish them 'and from that time he was never well so long as he lived'.

It was perhaps fortunate for the man who made this request, John Dee (1527–1608), that it was not granted. For some of the instructions he believed he had received from the supposed angels was of such a nature that it is unlikely that any court of the period would have thought it came from a heavenly source.

The man with cropped ears

John Dee seems to have been first suspected of knowing more about black magic than he ought when, in the 1540s, he was a student at Cambridge. By 1555, during the reign of Mary Tudor, suspicion had so increased that he spent some time in prison while a charge that he had attempted to use enchantments against the Queen was investigated.

Dee managed to clear himself of this accusation and during the early years of the reign of Queen Elizabeth I was in such high favour at court that on at least two occasions the Queen visited his home at Mortlake. By this time he already seems to have been trying to communicate with angelic beings, endeavouring to use ritual in order to induce spirits to manifest themselves through a 'magic mirror' or crystal. Dee himself seems to have had few psychic abilities. He saw little or

Dee's obsession with the spiritual and demonic magic which was practised widely in the 16th century was reflected in the complex symbolism of the frontispiece to his *Tuba Veneris*.

***Sigillum Dei Aemeth*, a wax tablet engraved by Dee and Kelley in accordance with instructions from 'spirit beings' and used in rites designed to invoke angels.**

Many of those scholars of the 16th and 17th century who endeavoured to enter into communication with superhuman beings protested that they were neither sorcerers nor demon worshippers. They were, so they said, practising 'angel magic', and the creatures with which they spoke were virtuous citizens of heaven not subjects of Satan.

One such practitioner of angel magic was so distressed by allegations of devil worship that in June 1604 he actually went to the length of petitioning King James I upon the matter. He wrote that he wished to be:

> . . . tried and cleared of that horrible and damnable . . . and defamatory slander . . . that he is or has been a Conjuror or Caller or Invocator of devils . . . [this] suppliant offers himself willingly to the punishment of Death (yea . . . to be stoned . . . or to be buried alive: or to be burned unmercifully) if . . . the said name of . . . Invocator of devils . . . can be duly . . . attributed to him.

nothing in his crystal and therefore employed seers, or 'scryers', to tell him what they saw and recount the words uttered by allegedly angelic voices.

The first seer whom Dee employed, a certain Barnabas Saul, proved unsatisfactory and was dismissed. The second, a mysterious young man with cropped ears, was to lead Dee into strange adventures.

Magician or trickster?

The young man called himself Edward Kelley, although his real name seems to have been Talbot, his ears had been lost as the result of a conviction for forgery, and he was a magician and seer – or confidence trickster – of genius.

The complicated angelic messages he gave to Dee were couched in high flown language but were often meaningless. Sometimes, however, they were very specific; on one occasion, for example, they included what were to prove very accurate prophecies of both the Spanish Armada and the execution of Mary, Queen of Scots.

Dee was completely convinced of the veracity of the messages and their angelic source. Following the instructions of his angelic guides he packed up much of his belongings and, in company with his young wife and

The magic mirror, or crystal, in which John Dee's clairvoyant, Edward Kelley, beheld the supposed angel who instructed them to sleep with each other's wives.

John Dee, at one time an adviser to Queen Elizabeth I on matters occult and astrological, who sought angelic wisdom and foretold the Spanish Armada and the execution of Mary Queen of Scots.

children, journeyed to Poland and Bohemia with Kelley.

There, in the unfamiliar world of eastern Europe, the angels gave Dee the instructions that would have convinced any English court that he was an 'invocator of devils'. He and Kelley were to share their wives with one another.

There is no doubt that the command was obeyed; a heavily scored out but legible passage in Dee's diary records the angel asking Dee whether Kelley's wife had been 'humble and obedient' to him on the previous night. Dee had answered 'yes'.

Dee parted from Kelley and returned to England. He died in 1608, poor and neglected, still seeking another seer. In his last years the questions asked by Dee of his supposed angels were mundane enough. One of his last enquiries, addressed to a being whom he believed to be the Archangel Raphael, was: 'Of the blood, not coming out of my Fundament [rectum], but at a little as it were pinhole of the skin . . .'. The Archangel, through the mouth of Dee's seer, promised a full recovery, which was never obtained.

Urban VIII, a member of the great Barberini family which gave many Cardinals to the Church, practised astrology and caused considerable irritation to the members of the College of Cardinals by making forecasts of impending doom.

The Church condemned almost all types of magic, even that supposedly concerned not with the denizens of hell but with angels and the spirits of the planets. The one exception – and even that was regarded with suspicion by some theologians – was what was referred to as natural magic. This was concerned with such matters as the secret, but in no way supernatural, properties of herbs, precious stones, minerals and substances of animal origin.

In 1586 Pope Sixtus v issued a proclamation, a Papal Bull, against all forms of magic and most forms of divination and fortune telling, while in 1592 even bishops and inquisitors were forbidden to read *grimoires* and other books dealing with such subjects.

Oddly enough several Popes were suspected of being practitioners of the very magic they condemned, amongst them being the one who had issued the proclamation of 1586. Sixtus v was probably innocent of the charges made against him, but there is no doubt that under a later Pope, Urban VIII, ritual magic was practised in the Vatican itself.

Magic cocktails

Urban VIII was a Pope with a firm belief in astrology who not only had horoscopes cast for his Cardinals but, on the basis of his perusal of those horoscopes, tactlessly informed some of these princes of the Church that they would shortly die. The heavenly aspects showed, so he told them, that the astral demons, the spirits of the planets, had decided to make an end of them.

The tables were turned during the period 1626–8 when a number of astrologers, possibly in the secret employ of irritated Cardinals, began to point out that evil aspects to Mars and Saturn indicated that the Pope's life was in danger. The alarmed Pope decided to protect himself by any means whatsoever and called in the aid of a magician.

This was Tommaso Campanella, a one time Dominican friar who had spent many years in a Neapolitan prison and was renowned for his knowledge of that variety of magic concerned with the planetary demons. Campanella and the Pope had several consultations and it was decided that a complicated ceremony involving the consumption of curious alcoholic potions, 'magical cocktails', should be performed immediately. This was because an impending eclipse of the sun increased the threat from the malignancy of the planetary demons of Mars and Saturn.

Jovial music

The planetary demons of Jupiter and Venus were considered by Campanella and the Pope to be as beneficial as those concerned with Mars and Saturn were evil. What was required, it was decided, was to reinforce the good jovial (Jupiterian) and Venusian influences.

Thomas Campanella, the Dominican friar who proclaimed that 'Jesus is my Doctrine' but practised the astrological white magic concerned with the demons, or perhaps angels, of the planets.

Two of the benefic 'planetary daemons' whose influence supposedly was attracted by Campanella and the Pope in the ceremonies they conducted are depicted here. On the right is the solar demon, on the left that of Venus.

In a sealed room hung with white silk Campanella and the Pope sprinkled rose vinegar, the rose being the sacred flower of the spirits of Venus, and burnt rosemary, laurel and other plants of good omen. They lighted two candles and five torches to symbolize the sun, moon and planets 'since the heavens, owing to the eclipse, were defective'. They played music considered appropriate to the astral demons of Jupiter and Venus in order to disperse 'the pernicious qualities of the eclipse-infected air'. Gems were used for the same purpose and magically distilled liquors, prepared from herbs believed to have occult properties, were drunk by the participants in the rite.

The magic was successful. The Pope lived on for another 16 years, dying in 1644, and Campanella himself survived until 1639. Nevertheless, the experience did nothing to induce the Pope to alleviate the Church's hostile attitude towards magic nor did it make him feel well disposed towards those who practised it. He sent Campanella to prison and, in 1631, issued a Bull against magic and divination. Stern punishments were ordered to be meted out to magicians who prophesied the deaths of princes, particularly Popes.

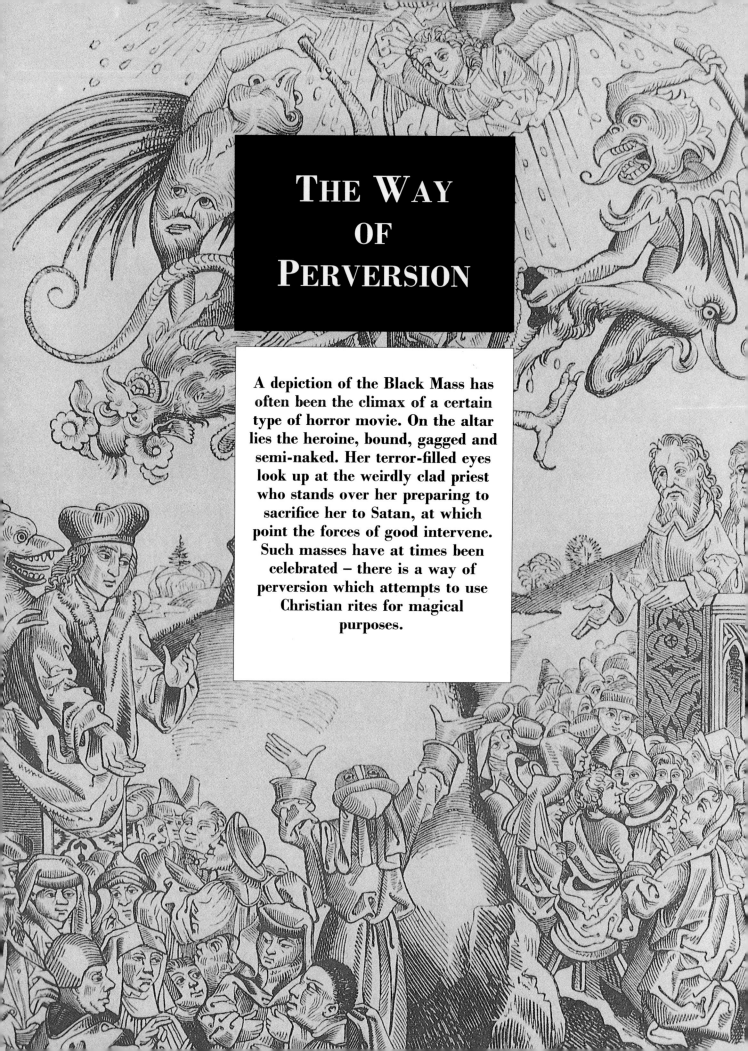

THE WAY OF PERVERSION

A depiction of the Black Mass has often been the climax of a certain type of horror movie. On the altar lies the heroine, bound, gagged and semi-naked. Her terror-filled eyes look up at the weirdly clad priest who stands over her preparing to sacrifice her to Satan, at which point the forces of good intervene. Such masses have at times been celebrated – there is a way of perversion which attempts to use Christian rites for magical purposes.

THE BLACK MASS

At one time the phrase 'black mass' had a perfectly respectable meaning, being no more than a popular term for a requiem mass, i.e., a mass said for the repose of the soul of a dead man or woman. In this connection the word 'black' was not used in the sense of 'evil' or 'averse' – it simply referred to the fact that it was customary to have black candles upon the alter during the celebration of such a mass.

The miracle of the mass

The mass, so it was and is believed by Catholic theologians, is in no sense a magical rite. It is held, however, to be a rite which involves a *miracle*, the 'transubstantiation' of the elements – the bread and wine – into the body and blood of Christ.

To understand what satanists and black magicians were doing, or believed that they were doing, when they performed their own blasphemous Black Masses, it must be understood exactly what is meant by the word 'transubstantiation'.

Following the Greek philosopher Aristotle, the scholastic philosophers of the Middle Ages taught that any material object had both 'substance' and 'accidents'. The latter were defined as all the attributes of an object which are perceptible to the human senses. Thus, the 'accidents' of an apple were defined as its taste, its colour, its size, shape and so on. These were not, however, regarded as the 'substance' of an apple, i.e., its essential 'appleness'. In other words, if an apple tree suddenly produced a fruit which was square, coloured grey and tasted like roast lamb, it would still be an apple – all the 'accidents' would have changed but not the 'substance', the quality of 'appleness'.

It is precisely the opposite process which Catholics believe to take place when a mass is celebrated. The bread and wine upon the altar are held to retain the accidents of bread and wine – the taste, appearance, and colour – but as they are no longer in substance bread and wine, they are held to be in substance the body and blood of Christ. This was, and is, believed in the most literal sense – the bread and wine regarded as being the body and blood of Christ as truly as were the physiological elements of the incarnate God who was crucified and rose from the dead.

Popular belief

In view of this teaching, it is not surprising that in medieval belief the mass was thought of as a magical rite

and the man who had the power of validly celebrating it, the ordained priest, was sometimes looked upon as being possessed of magical powers. It was not only simple, unlettered peasants who held beliefs of this sort. At least some priests believed that their priestly functions were quasi-magical and were prepared to use them for evil purposes; as early as the 7th century a Church Council condemned those priests who said a requiem mass for a living man with the intention of killing him.

In spite of this condemnation the practice went on – there are various references to it and similar abuses in medieval literature and, in 1500, the entire cathedral chapter of Cambrai celebrated masses against their Bishop, with whom they were in bitter conflict. From such malignant rites evolved the Black Mass of satanism.

A sorcerer, by his mitre an abbot or bishop, celebrates the black mass upon a woman's rump – more conventionally she would have lain face upwards.

According to the evidence given at a witch trial which took place in Aquitaine in 1594 a priest – or possibly the Devil – celebrated a mass wearing a cape with no cross upon it. For the usual elements, bread and wine, a piece of turnip and a chalice of water were substituted and the congregation of witches were sprinkled with stinking urine instead of holy water.

Like all stories given in evidence during witch trials this tale cannot be accepted uncritically as being factual. There is not the slightest doubt, however, that

In this picture the artist, who had attended many amatory masses and dabbled in magic, alchemy and bizarre sexuality, expressed his diabolic synthesis of them all.

in the 17th century blasphemous Black Masses were celebrated by some priests.

The best authenticated incidents of this sort took place during the reign of Louis XIV of France and there is no doubt that Madame de Montespan, mistress of the king and mother of three of his children, was involved in the matter. Further, there is some possibility that she actually participated in the rites and lay naked upon an altar while the celebrant, an aged priest, carried out various unpleasant manipulations of the consecrated host.

Doves' hearts

In 1667 Madame de Montespan decided to use sorcery in order to supplement her sexual attractions. She hired a priest named Mariette to celebrate two curious masses designed to hold the love of the King.

These 'amatory masses' were performed in orthodox style save that the Gospel was read over the head of Madame de Montespan and an incantation, or prayer, was recited asking that:

> . . . the Queen may be barren, that the King leave her table and bed for me, that I obtain from him all that I ask for myself and my relatives . . . that beloved and respected by great nobles I may be called to the councils of the King . . . that the Queen being repudiated I may marry the King.

A third and, in that it involved blood sacrifice, even more unorthodox mass followed. Two doves were symbolically identified with Louis XIV and Madame de Montespan – probably by being baptized with their names – and were bound upon the altar while mass was said over them. Finally their hearts were torn from their bodies. Quite how this spell was supposed to take effect is uncertain; it seems likely that the blood of the two birds was mingled together, perhaps in the chalice, thus symbolically uniting the vital forces, particularly those concerned with sexuality, of the King and his mistress.

Abortionist and witch

At first it seemed to Madame de Montespan that her love magic had succeeded. As time passed, however, it became apparent that while Louis XIV neglected his Queen he had neither the intention nor, indeed, the power to supplant her. Nor were Louis' desires for the

The pathway of perverse mysticism – the spiritual road that leads to the abyss rather than the heights – implied here was dominant amongst those who participated in amatory masses.

sexual services of his mistress always apparent and they seemed to wax and wane. It might be, feared Madame de Montespan, that far from supplanting the Queen she might herself be supplanted in the King's favour by a new mistress. Once again Madame de Montespan resorted to sorcery, taking as her adviser a sinister abortionist, poisoner and witch named La Voisin.

La Voisin's real name was Catherine Monvoisin. She was the mistress of a professional fortune teller named Le Sage, a man whose main source of income seems to

have been the sale of love philtres, which had been charged with magical power by being placed under the chalice during the celebration of mass. She also had a husband, a long suffering man who survived without complaint the many attempts made by his wife to poison him.

La Voisin was certainly a murderess and a sorceress. For money she was prepared to arrange for the celebration of the Black Mass in its most complete form, involving human sacrifice.

A MASS FOR ASMODEUS

Towards the end of 1678 Nicolas de la Reynie, Louis XIV's Lieutenant-General of Police, arrested a very large number of fortune tellers, sorcerers and priests who unquestionably had dabbled in black magic.

Amongst them were the infamous Catherine Monvoisin, occult adviser to Madame de Montespan, mistress of Louis XIV, and a 67-year-old priest named Guibourg, whom La Reynie described in the following terms:

> *A libertine who has travelled a great deal . . . and is at present attached to the Church of Saint Marcel. For twenty years he has engaged continually in the practice of poison, sacrilege and every evil business. He has cut the throats and sacrificed uncounted numbers of children on his infernal altar. He has a mistress . . . by whom he has had several children, one or two of whom he has sacrificed . . . It is no ordinary man who thinks it a natural thing to sacrifice infants by slitting their throats and to say Mass upon the bodies of naked women.*

The mass referred to was the Black Mass, a blasphemous deformation of the central rite of Christian worship, and it is likely that one of the naked women who served as a living altar for Guibourg's masses was Madame de Montespan, mother of three illegitimate children of Louis XIV.

Cantharides (Spanish fly)

From 1667 La Voisin had been supplying Madame de Montespan with love philtres. These had been introduced into the King's food with the objects of not only ensuring the monarch's continued affections for his favourite but of stimulating his sexual appetites. The ingredients of the philtres included a number of real and supposed aphrodisiacs, such as cantharides (Spanish fly) and the dried testicles of cockerels, which supposedly had been imbued with magical powers by Guibourg and other sorcerer priests. It seems likely that at least some of the mysterious illnesses which plagued Louis XIV during this period of his life resulted from the administration of these substances —

Guibourg, the debauched old priest who celebrated mass upon the bodies of naked women and sacrificed children to Asmodeus and other devils.

The mortuary mass

Over the following five years further Black Masses were celebrated. Nevertheless, by 1678 it was clear that Madame de Montespan was losing the King's favour and someone, probably one of the favourite's ladies-in-waiting, instructed Guibourg to celebrate a Black Mass designed to kill the King.

Under interrogation very full details of Guibourg's death spell were obtained by La Reynie, Louis XIV's police chief, from those who had participated. To the consecrated wine contained in the chalice were added semen, menstrual blood, dried powdered bats and, 'to give consistency', flour. This disgusting mess was taken away in a glass vial with the object of adding it to the King's food.

Before any further Black Masses could take place, La Voisin, Guibourg and no less than 216 other men and women suspected of sorcery or murder were in custody. Of these 110 were tried and sentenced – some hanged, some exiled, some imprisoned for life. The trials were brought to an end by the King – he was not prepared for the details of Madame de Montespan's activities to be made public. For some years the King simulated a continued friendship with her, but then retired her to the country.

The Marquise de Montespan, mistress of Louis XIV and mother of some of his children, on whose behalf magic was used to ensure the continuance of royal favour.

cantharides is a dangerous poison.

By 1673 love philtres and the amatory masses (*see* p. 108) were proving inadequate and, at the instigation of Madame de Montespan, La Voisin and Guibourg resorted to stronger and darker magic. A mass was celebrated on the body of a masked but otherwise naked woman, conceivably Madame de Montespan herself, and at the moment of the consecration of the bread and wine a child's throat was cut and its blood drained into the chalice. Simultaneously, a prayer was recited to the demons Ashtaroth and Asmodeus: 'Prince of Love, I beseech you to accept the sacrifice of this child . . . that the love of the King may be continued . . .'

LE PORTRAIT DE LA VOISIN.

Catherine Monvoisin ('La Voisin'), the sorceress, poisoner and abortionist, who supplied the black magician Guibourg with both his clients and his victims.

111

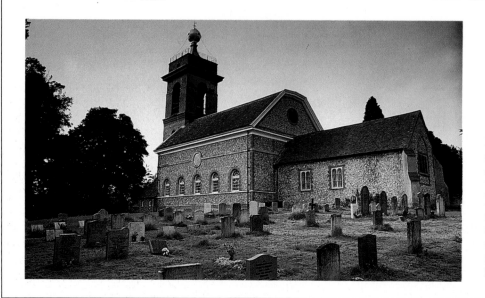

In the Golden Ball surmounting the Church of St Lawrence at West Wycombe, Sir Francis Dashwood and his associates in their mysterious society were accustomed to gather for purposes which they kept to themselves.

Some of those involved in the Black Mass scandals of the Paris of the 1670s lived on well into the 18th century. Louis XIV ordered that those who had not been formally tried and executed should be imprisoned for life under conditions which ensured that they did not talk. Above all, said an instruction sent to one prison governor:

> *. . . insist that the guards take measure to stop anyone hearing the nonsense that this gang is capable of saying. They have been known to speak infamies about Madame de Montespan . . . warn the prisoners that they will be mercilessly punished if they say the least word on such a subject.*

It was over 40 years before the last of these chained, silenced prisoners met his death. Madame de Montespan had herself died 14 years earlier; in old age she had been noted for her seeming piety and for her fear of darkness, solitude and, above all, death.

Adolescent blasphemy

Any priests who celebrated the Black Mass, worshipped Satan, or practised sorcery in 18th-century France kept a very low profile indeed, and there are no well-authenticated reports of the activities of such men. There are, however, stories of deliberate acts of blasphemy, but such acts seem to have been inspired by a desire to flaunt a personal contempt for the Church and its teachings rather than any real belief in Satan, his cohorts and the efficacy of magic, black or white.

In 18th-century Ireland, Scotland and England similar acts of adolescent blasphemy were reliably reported. Thus, for example, George Augustus Selwyn, from whose sister, Albinia, is descended the present Duchess of York, was sent down from Oxford for uttering the phrase 'Do this in remembrance of me' – the words used by Jesus at the Last Supper – after downing a brimming flagon of wine in a tavern. This incident has led some to assert that Selwyn was a practising satanist. There is, in fact, no real evidence for this assertion, although Selwyn certainly did some very odd things in the course of his life – his favourite recreations were attending public executions and looking at corpses. He was also suspected of being a member of the Hellfire Club, a curious group centred round Sir Francis Dashwood (1708–81) which acquired a dark reputation which probably was undeserved.

Brimstone Boys

Dashwood's society only became referred to as the Hellfire Club some years after his death. Probably, it was given this name because of vague memories of a 'Hellfire Club' which operated in Dublin in the early decades of the 18th century. Like similar Irish societies of the same period, such as the 'Brimstone Boys' and the 'Blue Blazers', there is no reason to believe that its members engaged in anything more diabolical than wenching, heavy drinking and making coarse jokes at the expense of the pious.

The proceedings of the 'Medmenham Monks', as Dashwood and his associates were referred to during the heyday of their activities, the years from 1750 to 1762, were probably very similar if more decorous. Each June the 'monks' gathered for two or three weeks at the Dashwood home, Medmenham Abbey, where they dined, got drunk, engaged in sexual junketings with women ironically termed 'nuns', and, so it would seem, on occasion performed some sort of rituals in the Abbey's chapel. It has been suggested that these rituals were Black Masses. This, as Mr Eric Towers has pointed out, is extremely unlikely. From the known opinions of Dashwood and his fellows, it seems more probable that they were only half-serious pagan ceremonies involving the worship of Venus.

Dashwood cannot be considered an authentic satanist – but one can be sure that the satanic tradition was alive in his time and that it surfaced in the following century.

Sir Francis Dashwood, at one time Chancellor of the Exchequer, was the guiding spirit of the 'Medmenham Monks', whose strange revels led to them being referred to as the Hellfire Club.

Dashwood as depicted by Hogarth in a portrait commissioned by members of the Dilettanti Society. He was jokingly portrayed as a Franciscan friar blasphemously engaged in the worship of Venus.

The occultist Saint-Yves d'Alveydre, a one-time admirer of Vintras who endeavoured to conceal his intellectual indebtedness to the latter and claimed to have been taught by 'a high official of the Brahmin Church'.

In 1839 Eugene Vintras, the foreman of a cardboard box factory at Tilly-sur-Seule, received a letter, or believed that he received a letter, from the Archangel Michael. This letter contained, said Vintras, 'a refutation of heresy and a profession of Catholic orthodoxy'.

While the Archangel wrote no further letters to Vintras he, and even the Blessed Virgin and St Joseph, presented themselves in vision to Vintras. They told him that he was the reincarnation of the Prophet Elijah, that his task was to proclaim to the world a coming Age of the Holy Ghost, that he was to found a new religious body, 'the Work of Mercy', and that a man named Charles Naundorf was the rightful King of France.

There is no reason to doubt the sincerity of Vintras, who was clearly deluded rather than fraudulent, and he spent the rest of his life in attempting to obey the heavenly instructions he believed he had been given.

Mystic bloodstains

Vintras was an unlettered man, but his deep personal conviction made him a powerful preacher. He travelled round France preaching universal redemption and the coming kingship of Naundorf who, so he said, was the son of Louis XVI and Marie Antoinette. Soon he acquired a following which included a few eccentric priests, notably the Abbé Charvoz, who rapidly became the theologian of the 'Work of Mercy'.

At Tilly the priests, who accepted the genuineness of the mission which Vintras claimed to have been given, set up an oratory. There, clad in curious vestments, they celebrated a strange mass which they called the *Provictimal Sacrifice of Mary* and witnessed, so they said, many curious events, some of them reminiscent of the strangest tales told in the Middle Ages.

They saw, for example, empty chalices brimming with blood; they saw strangely shaped mystic bloodstains appear on the consecrated bread; they saw the Holy Ghost in the form of a fat pigeon perch on Vintras' shoulder during a celebration of the Eucharist.

The experiences which the congregations at Tilly believed they had undergone were matched by the increasingly lurid visions of hell which Vintras himself experienced. Thus, in May 1841, he saw:

. . . on every side an abyss full of hideous monsters who called me brother . . . Suddenly great whirlpools of flame arose from the abyss into which I was about to fall. I heard yells of furious exultation . . .

The Polish mathematician and occultist Hoene Wronski developed a curious Messianic theology which was in part derived from the teachings of Vintras and his followers.

ly with an unfrocked priest named Boullan, a sinister and perverted individual who had celebrated not only the Black Mass but had almost certainly carried out a human sacrifice.

Vintras, depicted here celebrating an unorthodox Mass called 'the Provictimal Sacrifice of Mary' wore an inverted cross upon his vestments; this alone led many to regard him as a satanist.

Vintras was saved from the abyss by the Virgin. Nothing, however, served to save him from the attention of the ecclesiastical authorities, who were growing increasingly alarmed by the eccentric nature of the masses celebrated by him and his followers.

Magical prayer

In 1841, the Bishop of Bayeux denounced the pamphlets published by Vintras' followers as being contrary to the Catholic faith. Seven years later the Church of Carmel, as Vintras' movement had become known, was condemned formally by the Pope. In 1851, Vintras' difficulties were increased when a former disciple published a pamphlet in which he accused the prophet of homosexuality and of celebrating weird Black Masses at which both priest and congregation were totally naked. At about the same time a man who had once been one of Vintras' priests publicly claimed that Vintras had taught him a 'magical prayer', which he was told to recite while masturbating at the altar.

In spite of these and similar attacks, Vintras' Church of Carmel survived and attracted a modest following which remained faithful until the prophet's death in 1875. Shortly before that event, Vintras became friend-

The Abbé Boullan, born in 1824, had a short but remarkable career as a Catholic priest. Not long after his 30th birthday he had become the confessor of a nun named Adèle Chevalier whom he quickly made his mistress. Adèle left her convent and, after bearing her lover at least two children, founded with him a group which they called 'The Society for the Reparation of Souls'.

The activities of this society reflected an obsession with devils, Satan worship and demonic possession which was to last throughout Boullan's entire life. It specialized in exorcism, the casting out of demons, using methods which were not only unorthodox but repellent to any believing Catholic. On one occasion,

for example, Boullan and his mistress purported to exorcize a group of supposedly possessed women by feeding them a disgusting mixture of human excrement and the consecrated host.

Ritual sacrifice

To defile the host in this way was to replicate some of the noxious techniques used by Guibourg almost 200 years earlier (*see* p. 110) and there is very strong evidence that, like Guibourg, Boullan celebrated the Black Mass. According to a document which survives in the Vatican archives, Boullan and his mistress celebrated on 8 January 1860 a Black Mass which incorporated

A human sacrifice at the climax of a Black Mass as depicted in the film *The Devil Rides Out*, adapted from Denis Wheatley's bestselling occult novel of the same name.

The decadent French artist Felicien Rops was influenced deeply by the erotic mysticism of Boullan and much of his work, as here in which the themes of rampant sexuality and demonic intervention are combined.

Bestiality

Documents survive which provide evidence that Boullan and his disciples engaged, or imagined that they engaged, in sexual activities with not only angels and other heavenly beings but with the spirits of the mighty dead – Cleopatra and Alexander the Great, for example.

The techniques used to achieve these ghostly copulations were largely masturbatory, the man or woman concerned was simply fantasizing that he or she was having sexual intercourse with a disembodied being. On occasion a human partner, also a member of the Church of Carmel, was involved. In this case each would imagine the other to be an angel.

Boullan also seems to have approved of bestiality, sexual relationships between animals and human beings, on the grounds that it speeded up the spiritual evolution of the animals concerned. There is no hard evidence that he acted on this theory, but some of his followers may have done so.

Such teachings as those described above were only given to those in the inner circle of Boullan's so-called Church. In public he posed as a man of great, if eccentric, piety.

The Abbé Boullan, fictionalized in J.K. Huymans' novel *Là Bas* as the saintly 'Doctor Johannes', was in reality a practitioner of sexual magic and the murderer of his own child.

the ritual sacrifice of their own bastard child.

Subsequently, Boullan claimed to be the reincarnation of St John the Baptist and the successor of the prophet Vintras as head of the tiny Church of Carmel. As such he taught his followers a number of sexual techniques which were described as allowing 'men and women to enter into carnal union with heavenly beings'. In other words, he was advocating a mating between human beings and creatures similar to the *incubi* and *succubi* described by the demonologists of the Middle Ages and the Renaissance.

Boullan held that the sin of Adam and Eve which had led to their expulsion from the Garden of Eden had been sexual in nature and, paradoxically, that redemption could be achieved – original sin wiped out – through sexuality. He claimed that:

> ... as the Fall had been caused by a culpable act of love it is through acts of love accomplished in a religious spirit that the Redemption of humanity can be achieved.

If men and women copulated with angels and archangels, said Boullan, they would climb a spiritual ladder which ultimately would lead them to a mystic union with God.

Boullan, Supreme Pontiff of the Church of Carmel in his own estimation, a satanist and black magician in that of almost everyone else who knew the real nature of his teachings, died in 1893 at the height of a 'witch war', a sort of battle between rival groups of magicians.

The initiator of the war was Stanislas de Guaita, a minor writer who had abandoned literature for magic. His life from 1885, the year of his conversion to occultism, until his death in 1897 was devoted to 'reviving the ancient mysteries', struggling against the machinations of black magicians, real or supposed, and 'projecting the astral body'. The latter he believed he achieved as a result of taking very large doses of hashish, cocaine and morphine.

Pontiff of infamy

In 1888, de Guaita became aware of the real nature of Boullan's teachings and denounced the 'Supreme

Huysmans, participant in the amazing astral battles of the French magicians of the 1890s, began his literary career as a realist, went on to write such decadent novels as *À Rebours* and *Là Bas*, and ended his life as a devout Catholic.

Pontiff' as: 'a priest of infamy, a base idol of the mystical Sodom, a magician of the worst type, a wretched criminal and an evil sorcerer'.

De Guaita did not keep his opinions to himself. He not only publicized them but sent Boullan a letter informing him that he was a 'condemned man' – a phrase which both Boullan and his friend J.K. Huysmans interpreted as a threat to commit some sort of magical murder.

Soon both Boullan and Huysmans were claiming that they were the victims of evil spells. The latter wrote to his friends to tell them that he was the victim of what he called 'fluidic fisticuffs' – both he and, ludicrously, his cat suffered blows from invisible demons. Huysmans' countermeasures included burning an incense compounded by Boullan and reciting conjurations 'dissolving the astral fluids and paralysing the powers of the sorcerers'.

On 3 January 1893, Boullan wrote to Huysmans informing him that on the previous night he had felt a sense of suffocation and in the morning 'a black bird of death cried out'. On the evening of the same day Boullan collapsed and died, presumably as the result of a heart attack.

Stanislas de Guaita, magician and poet, was the founder of the French occult group from which was derived the Catholic Rose-Croix, responsible for the exhibition advertised here.

A supremely powerful spell

Huysmans was convinced that Boullan's death was not a natural one. He gave an interview to a newspaper in which he asserted that:

. . . de Guaita and his friends practise black magic every day. Poor Boullan was engaged in perpetual conflict with the evil demons they continually sent him from Paris . . . . It is quite possible that my poor friend Boullan has succumbed to a supremely powerful spell.

Infuriated by both Huysmans' accusation and a similar one made by Jules Bois, an occult writer who had once been a member of the Church of Carmel, de Guaita challenged both men to a duel. Huysmans had no stomach for a fight and apologized. However, Bois decided to fight, informing one of his friends that he would 'see something singular . . . on both sides our allies are praying for us and practising conjurations'. Whether as a result of conjurations or bad marksmanship, the duel ended in farce rather than tragedy. Only one of the antagonists succeeded in firing his pistol and he missed his opponent.

Three days later another duel was fought and this time the sorcery seems to have been more effective – the horse taking Bois to the duelling ground mysteriously collapsed throwing him violently to the ground. Nevertheless, the duel took place, both men suffering minor injuries.

Shortly afterwards, honour being satisfied, the two sides became reconciled with one another. The witch war, which had been fought with both conjurations and more physical weapons, was at an end.

By the time this drawing was executed Huysmans was a pious Catholic; only a few years before he had attended the Black Mass and, in his own words, 'dwelt in privies'.

119

HELLISH RENAISSANCE

It was not only the Black Mass and the invocation of devils which were revived in the 19th century. There was also an occult renaissance, a rebirth of beliefs concerning demons, magic and witchcraft which at the end of the previous century had been regarded as relics of the Middle Ages.

The revival began in France, rapidly spread to England and other countries and has been the fount from which has originated modern occultism, both black and white.

Bulwer Lytton's friend, Levi, had a curious conception of the nature of evil. As illustrated in this symbolic drawing he saw Satan as being, so to speak, the shadow of God.

In both England and France there were faint stirrings of interest in ritual magic at the very beginning of the 19th century. But the key event which sparked off the modern revival of interest in ritual magic, witchcraft and demonology was the publication in 1856 of a book devoted to what its author called 'High Magic'.

The author in question was Eliphas Levi (1810–75), the son of a poor cobbler, who had trained for the priesthood but abandoned the Church for occultism, a subject in which he was widely read although in no sense a scholar.

Even before he had published anything on the subject of demons and magic, black or white, Levi had established a reputation for himself as a 'mage' – a master magician. He retained this reputation throughout his lifetime and even after his death; at the present

day his books are still in print and are studied avidly by those present day occultists who desire to make the personal acquaintance of unseen beings.

A Rosicrucian

It is surprising that Levi enjoyed such a high reputation as a practising ritual magician, for he only ever seems to have performed one magical operation in his entire life. It took place in England, not Levi's native France, and was carried out at the instigation of an English novelist and politician, Edward Bulwer Lytton, created Baron Lytton of Knebworth in 1863.

Lytton was the author of *Zanoni* (1842), a novel concerning the doings of a master magician who was a member of some secret and enormously powerful occult society, perhaps the legendary Rosicrucian brotherhood. As a result of his authorship of *Zanoni* Lytton was regarded as an authority on magic and allied subjects. Some even thought that he was himself a Rosicrucian, and in a sense this was true, for he was undoubtedly a member of at least two secret societies which called themselves Rosicrucian.

Evocation

Levi journeyed to London in 1854, hoping to give lessons in occultism and equipped with a letter of introduction to Lytton. The visit was not a success. Few, if any, pupils presented themselves to Levi and he was pestered, as he himself complained, to 'perform miracles'. In other words, he was asked to evoke demons and other spirits to visible appearance. While he would not, or could not, do this in the presence of others he did agree to perform some solitary evocations in order to provide answers to questions which were troubling the mind of a friend of Lytton's.

Levi gave a detailed description of the four evocations of the spirit he chose to call upon, that of Apollonius, the semi-divine Greek magician of antiquity. After complicated rituals the figure of Apollonius appeared and answered the two questions, the exact content of which Levi did not choose to reveal, asked by Lytton's friend. Both answers were gloomy, one of them being the single word 'Death'.

Seven years later Lytton, carried out further invocations but no details of them are known. Levi continued his occult career; Lytton became a leading politician and 'Grand Patron' of a masonic body which called itself 'the Rosicrucian Society' in England.

DEMONS WITH HALF-GNAWED FACES

A symbolic design, painted by MacGregor Mathers' wife Moina, sister of the philosopher Henri Bergson, for the use of initiates of the inner Rosicrucian group of the Hermetic Order of the Golden Dawn.

One day in the 1890s an aristocratic lady occultist engaged S.L. MacGregor Mathers, a leading member of the Rosicrucian Society, in conversation on the subject of the demons who, so she said, infested her bedroom.

These demons, she claimed, resembled corpses with half-gnawed faces and they continually asked her to allow them to enter her bed, a request which she found it difficult to refuse. What, she enquired, did Mr Mathers think of it?

'Shocking bad taste on both sides', barked Mathers, and there the matter has rested!

Dedicated magicians, such as Mathers, are not usually noted for their sense of humour, and this was the only joke that he was ever recorded as making. This is not surprising; his life was full of too much demonic and white magic for him to have much time to spare for anything else.

Golden Dawn

Mathers, born in 1854, had become fascinated by the magic of the *grimoires* (see page 93) as a very young man and in 1889 published an English translation of the *Clavicula Salomonis*, which he seriously believed to have been written by King Solomon. This version of the famous *grimoire* was heavily expurgated – Mathers regarded himself as a white magician and cut out most of the processes involving blood sacrifice or intended to produce immoral results. Notably *sexually* immoral results – Mathers regarded sexual activity as undesirable in itself and he and his wife, the sister of the philosopher Henri Bergson, never consummated their marriage.

Mathers was the most prominent member of an occult secret society called the Golden Dawn, in which ritual magic and the 'medieval occult sciences' were taught in the higher grades, largely on the basis of manuscripts compiled by Mathers himself.

Some of these manuscripts were compiled from printed and manuscript sources to be found in the British Museum and other great libraries. Others, generally the most interesting, were derived, so Mathers claimed, from superhuman beings whom he called 'the Masters' or 'the Secret Chiefs'. By the latter phrase he meant that the Golden Dawn had a hidden leadership of which he was the representative; he claimed that these beings, whom he had on rare occasions met, were 'human and living on this earth but possessing terrible superhuman powers'.

Opposing demonic forces

Mathers rarely encountered these mysterious instructors on the physical plane and most of the instructions he received from them was delivered by more occult methods which he found terribly exhausting. He described his efforts and their results:

Mathers' disciple Frater Iehi Aour (real name Alan Bennett), who in 1896 carried out, in company with actress Florence Farr, a staggeringly complex ceremony designed to evoke the spirit of Mercury to visible appearance.

. . . by clairvoyance – by astral projection . . . at times by direct voice audible to my ears and those of Vestigia [Mathers' wife] . . . The strain of such labour has been enormous . . . the nerve prostration after each reception being terrible . . . accompanied by . . . severe loss of blood from the mouth, nose, and occasionally the ears . . . Add to all this the Ceremonies of Evocation, almost constant strife with opposing Demonic Forces . . .

W.B. Yeats knew Mathers well and in later life was to refer to him as 'half lunatic, half knave'. Yeats also studied magic and the curious symbol systems taught in the manuscripts compiled by Mathers and had no doubt of his teacher's sincerity. Mathers, he said, was a man who only half-lived in the ordinary world of physical events and had difficulty in differentiating between objective happenings and those psychological states of which he had interior experiences.

Nevertheless, whether Mathers ever did meet the superhuman beings he claimed to have encountered or not, there is no doubt that he formulated a complex and logical structure of magical techniques which enabled his followers – or so they believed – to protect themselves from demons and vampires.

MacGregor Mathers, magician and seer, wearing what he thought of as 'Egyptian vestments' while publicly conducting the worship of Isis in a Parisian theatre of the 1890s.

Dr Berridge, a homoeopathic physician who claimed to have experienced a number of meetings with vampires, found the magical and visualization processes outlined in the manuscripts compiled by Mathers to be extremely useful in coping with these creatures.

Berridge's interpretation of the activities of vampires was rather more subtle than that popularized in such tales as Bram Stoker's *Dracula*. He did not believe they merely sucked blood from their victims but the life force itself. They were human beings, so he believed, who charged themselves with vital energy by drawing it from other people, who might be friends, relations, or total strangers.

Berridge's technique for dealing with the vampires he encountered was to surround himself with what he called 'odic fluid', a mysterious substance which Mathers and others believed to be halfway between the worlds of matter and spirit and was more commonly referred to as 'the astral light'.

A fidgety old vampire

Vampires, Berridge believed, could take the most surprising forms – on one occasion he encountered a vampire whose outward appearance was that of 'a prosy fidgety old gentleman'.

Berridge seems to have known the old gentleman well – perhaps he was one of his patients – and had a number of prolonged meetings with him. These Berridge found peculiarly and alarmingly exhausting and he decided that he was, in his own words, 'being preyed upon by a man of exhausted nervous vitality'. The man was not, said Berridge, a *conscious* vampire, but in his innermost self was an intentional vampire, for in spite of his advanced age he intended to marry a young girl in order to 'recuperate his exhausted vitality'. Berridge writes of the next time the arrival of the supposed vampire was announced, presumably by a servant:

> . . . [I] closed myself to him before he was admitted. I imagined that I had formed myself a complete investiture of odic fluid, surrounding me on all sides, but not touching me, and impenetrable to any hostile currents. This magical process was immediately and permanently successful – I never had to repeat it.

Berridge used similar measures to deal with various elementals – demons of a very low order – whom he

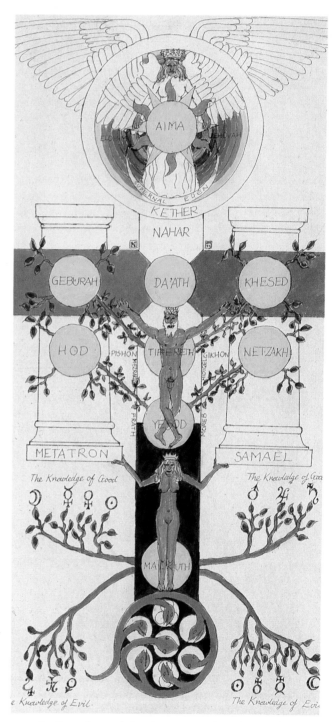

Dr Berridge and Brodie Innes believed that the psychic vampirism with which they concerned themselves was an outcome of the activities of the demonic forces known as 'the shells' and was symbolized in this diagram by the seven-headed serpent at the foot of the cross.

encountered at various times in his life. Friends of Berridge, amongst them a certain J.W. Brodie Innes, also believed they were subject to attack by these malignant creatures.

A foul shape

Brodie Innes and his wife were suffering from what seemed to them a more than natural exhaustion and came to the conclusion that they were being obsessed by what they called a vampirizing elemental.

To banish it Brodie Innes decided to evoke it to visible manifestation, using various mystic names and symbols he had learned from Mathers and his instructional manuscripts. Immediately a vague blot, like a scrap of thick fog, became visible; reciting magical words of power Brodie Innes ordered the demon to manifest itself more fully. He then saw, at first dimly but then with complete clarity, 'a most foul shape, between a bloated big-bellied toad and a malicious ape'.

Brodie Innes projected all his psychic strength against the demon. He felt a sense of shock and a momentary dimness of vision – and then the thing was gone, leaving behind nothing but a foul smell.

Both the magician and his wife immediately recovered their normal vitality and health.

According to MacGregor Mathers, whom Brodie Innes consulted on this curious matter, the entity which had been destroyed was not a single elemental but many, who somehow had combined to form one powerful devil.

The 'serpent of wisdom', a traditional symbol which Berridge and Brodie Innes believed symbolized the upward path from the world of matter to the world of pure spirit.

This 19th-century engraving of a vampire and its victim implicitly conveys the links between the concepts of sexual energy and vampirism – the occultist Brodie Innes referred to an elderly vampire taking a young wife in order to restore his energies.

125

THE DEMONS BUER AND CHORONZON

MacGregor Mathers taught his magic to many people, some who were to spend their lives in obscurity, others who were to become famous or notorious. The most notable of the latter was Aleister Crowley, a man who had few disciples during his lifetime but has a considerable cult following at the present day.

Crowley was born in 1875, the son of parents who were fanatical members of an extreme Protestant sect and believed in the literal truth of every word in the Bible. While still an adolescent Crowley rejected his parents' beliefs and for the rest of his life remained bitterly anti-Christian – so much so that he identified himself with the Beast 666, the devilish monster whose iniquities are described in Revelations, the final book of the New Testament.

In 1898 Crowley was initiated into Mathers' society and between then and 1900 made a rapid upwards progress through its degrees of initiation. As well as what he learned of magic from the instructional documents compiled by Mathers he had a personal tutor in practical occultism, a brilliant young engineer named Alan Bennett.

Crowley dressed in the vestments he wore as head of the magical society he founded called the 'A.∴ A.∴', these being the initials of the Latin words meaning 'Silver Star'.

Alan Bennett, Aleister Crowley's first teacher in practical magic. It was in order to raise money for Bennett that Crowley 'evoked the demon Buer to visible appearance' in his Chancery Lane flat.

A design by J.F.C. Fuller, a one-time disciple of Crowley who later became a Major-General and a personal friend of Adolf Hitler, for the decoration of a planned Crowleyan temple.

Black and white temples

In Crowley's London flat he and Bennett worked at magic in two rooms referred to as 'the white and the black temples'. The second of these contained a weird altar supported by a wooden image of a black man standing on his hands and a skeleton anointed with blood from the sparrows which Crowley sacrificed to it.

The white temple contained an altar and other 'magical furniture', was lined with mirrors, and was dedicated to the more innocent aspects of practical occultism. Even so it seems to have been productive of a sinister psychic atmosphere.

On one evening in 1899 Crowley and his friend Jones, also a practising magician, went out for dinner, locking up the white temple before they did so. On their return they found the locked door open, the altar overthrown and magical symbols strewn about the room.

They restored the white temple to its proper order and then, clairvoyantly one supposes, observed that semi-materialized demons were processing around the room.

In the same year Crowley and Jones decided to 'evoke to visible appearance' a demon named Buer — a creature described in a 16th-century magical text as teaching philosophy, healing all distempers, and governing 50 legions of the spirits of hell. The operation was only partly successful; outside the protective magic circle in which stood Crowley and Jones appeared a misty warrior-like figure of which only part of the leg and the helmet were clearly visible.

A mighty devil

Crowley seems to have found the classical techniques of demon evocation somewhat long-winded and there is no evidence that he used them after the partial appearance of Buer. In 1909, however, he actually seems to have carried out an occult ritual designed to get Choronzon, described in a 16th-century text as 'that mighty devil', to occupy his own body temporarily.

This rite was performed in the North African desert, Crowley's co-worker being his disciple Victor Neuburg. The latter sat within a protective magic circle, Crowley within a triangle in which he had sacrificed three pigeons.

After an invocation of Choronzon had been recited Neuburg began to see curious things within the triangle in which Crowley sat — a seductive woman, a serpent, an old man, a murderous madman, and so on.

Eventually Choronzon was banished by Neuburg, who for the rest of his life remained convinced that he literally had encountered a demon. Perhaps he had, even if that demon had operated through Crowley's body.

In this symbolic design J.F.C. Fuller expressed his tantric (magical/sexual) interpretation of the polarity between the 'female' zodiacal circle and the uprush of the 'male' forces of the physical world.

The techniques of the modern magicians, black and white, who base their occult rituals on the teachings of such men as Eliphas Levi, MacGregor Mathers and Aleister Crowley bear an astonishing resemblance to some aspects of the Brazilian spirit-magic known as 'Macumba'.

Strictly speaking there is no such thing as Macumba; it is a collective term for cults which are more correctly referred to as Candomblé, Umbanda and Quimbanda.

The first of these, Candomblé, is derived directly from the African religions, magic and witchcraft brought to Brazil by the hundreds of thousands of slaves who were transported there between the 16th and 19th centuries. Umbanda has evolved from a blend of influences derived from both Candomblé and Euro-

pean spiritualism and magic, while Quimbanda is black magic, performed by devotees of Lucifer and the unclean spirits who are his subjects.

Most of the slaves brought to Brazil came from those parts of West Africa dominated by the Yoruba peoples, and with them they brought a belief in the gods and goddesses of the Yoruba – in Olorum, king of the gods; in Shango, god of the thunder; and in Yemanja, originally looked upon as no more than an ocean goddess but now regarded by many Macumba devotees as being the queen of heaven.

Divine possession

The central feature of the rites of Macumba is divine

In the Brazilian state of Amazonia, a Macumba priest enters the trance state during which his body will be controlled by the demi-god known as the Old Black Slave.

King Exú's servants

Quimbanda, the dark aspect of the Macumba family of magical religions, is a sinister witchcraft relating to those demons who follow Lucifer, often referred to by Macumba devotees as King Exú. Lucifer's chief assistants are believed to be Beelzebub and Ashtaroth, popularly known as Exú Mor and Exú of the Crossroads. These are thought to command a host of minor devils, of whom Exú of the Closed Paths is the most dreaded.

To get this being to act against someone a Quimbanda practitioner will prepare a red satin cloth adorned with mystic symbols and take it to a crossroads. On it he places four red and black crosses, a plucked but uncooked cockerel stuffed with red pepper, and other objects. He then lights 13 candles, reciting at the same time the name of his enemy.

If the ceremony has been effective the enemy will 'find all paths closed'. The victim will become jobless, be unlucky in love, and suffer a host of illnesses. It is believed that such a one can only be cured, have the paths reopened, by employing the services of one of the gods who manifest themselves at Macumba rites.

The priest, now in full trance, is believed to be the Old Black Slave incarnate. As such, he uses his healing powers upon a sick child.

Beaches near Rio de Janeiro are a favourite place for Macumba devotees to make offerings to Yemanja, the merciful sea goddess whom some identify with the Virgin Mary.

possession; some of the worshippers enter into a trance which is believed to indicate that their bodies have been taken over by the beings they worship. The basic techniques used to induce these trance states are dancing, rhythmic drumming and a deliberate over-breathing. This unquestionably causes changes in brain chemistry which may be largely responsible for some of the seemingly supernormal feats performed by possessed worshippers – for example, walking on broken glass, extinguishing burning torches in their mouths and drinking enormous quantities of raw cane spirit without becoming noticeably drunken.

To an outsider witnessing a Macumba rite the events which proceed and succeed possession seem spontaneous, almost chaotic. In fact they are patterned, and someone possessed by a particular god or goddess will behave in the way that is dictated by Macumba tradition. Thus a woman possessed by a god known as 'the Old Black Slave' will adopt a crippled posture, smoke a pipe and massage the sick – the Old Black Slave is renowned for his healing powers.

129

The dance that induces the *loa* – the gods and goddesses of the voodoo faith – to 'mount', i.e. to possess the minds of devotees of the cult which still dominates much of rural Haiti.

Voodoo is sometimes thought of as no more than the variety of black magic and witchcraft practised in Haiti. In fact it is an authentic folk religion, a blend of elements derived from African spirit worship, European magic and popular Catholicism, and its central feature is identical with that of Brazilian Macumba – divine possession.

For the voodoo devotee the gods and goddesses have a quality of *closeness*. They descend to earth and take over the bodies of ordinary human beings who temporarily become divine. The entranced, supposedly possessed, worshipper transcends the human condition, is for a time unconscious of the hardship of ordinary life and in a sense brings heaven or hell to his or her fellow worshippers.

There is much magic, black and white, which has become integrated into voodoo and, to the annoyance of the Church, voodoo devotees tend to regard Catholic ceremonies and the objects used in them as being possessed of powerful magical properties.

Virgin of the Palms

A Haitian peasant once remarked to an enquiring anthropologist that 'the things of the Church are always affairs of magic'. Catholic priests in Haiti are well aware of this belief and have often taken elaborate precautions against the theft of the consecrated host, altar candles, ecclesiastical vestments, flowers placed before the image of a saint and even splinters from the altar. For it is supposed that if some or all of these are utilized in a magic spell, good or evil, the power of the Church will become involved in the sorcery.

Even some festivals of the Church have been partially taken over for magical purposes, and supposedly Catholic pilgrims to the annual Haitian festival of the Virgin of the Palms have been observed worshipping Baron Samedi, the voodoo god known as 'lord of the cemeteries'.

Baron Samedi is considered to be a master of dark magic, particularly of those aspects of it concerned with corpses, graves and other unpleasant things, and he is associated with the curiously sexual *culte des morts*, the cult of the dead, to which the Haitian clergy are bitterly opposed.

The enclosure which surrounds a voodoo temple, and in which many ceremonies take place, is often centred upon a large tree, sacred to the serpent god Damballah.

The spirit religions of Africa such as those practised in the Congo, Benin and Togo exerted a strong formative influence on the development of Haitian voodoo.

Black and purple

The great festival of the Haitian cult of the dead takes place on All Souls' Day when Baron Samedi's worshippers, mostly women, clad themselves in black and purple and discreetly make their way to isolated cemeteries.

Some become entranced and possessed by either Baron Samedi himself or by his assistant Ghede, a minor god who is the 'grave digger', the bringer of death, of voodoo mythology. As Baron Samedi or Ghede they are worshipped by their fellow cultists who sing to them extremely indecent songs with a grossly sexual content and dance the *banda* in their honour. The banda is perhaps the most lascivious but least romantic of the world's dances and at the festivals of the

cult of the dead it is sometimes performed entirely by women, some of whom use large sticks to represent the erect male organ.

The American journalist W.B. Seabrook, a one time friend of Aleister Crowley, once attended a private ceremony held by members of the cult of the dead and described what he saw in his book *Magic Island*. While Seabrook always wrote dramatically, and while he often misunderstood the real nature of the voodoo rites he witnessed, there is no reason to doubt his claim that on the altar were human bones and that the priestess spoke in a voice 'resembling the prolonged death-rattle from a windpipe choked with phlegm or blood'. Such a voice is associated with the physical manifestations of Baron Samedi by whom the priestess was presumably possessed and who is believed by some Haitian Catholics to be just another name for Satan.

Archbishop Milingo, surrounded by European admirers, carries out an exorcism
in the church of Santa Maria Adolorata, the only Catholic place of worship in
which he is authorized to officiate.

As in the past, so in the present day the Catholic Church teaches the reality of Satan, hell and demonic intervention in human affairs. As such it accepts that, on occasion, men and women can become possessed by devils. In both Brazil and Haiti, a good many Catholic priests argue that at least some of those supposedly 'possessed by the gods' at the rites of Macumba and voodoo are not deluded but are genuinely possessed – by demons, not by God.

As a consequence of Catholic belief in the reality of demon possession the modern Church carries out exorcisms in exactly the same way, theologically speaking, as it did a thousand years ago. The Church is well aware, however, that many supposed victims of diabolical possession are fraudulent publicity seekers, hysterics, or sufferers from severe mental illness. As a result of this no Catholic priest is allowed to undertake exorcism without the authority of his Bishop, who will not give such permission unless he feels assured that

there is a strong possibility of the supposed possession being authentic. It is also usual for the Bishop who authorizes exorcism to issue instructions that the ceremony must be carried out in strict privacy.

Ashtaroth and the Archbishop

There are still, however, some Catholic bishops who are prepared to carry out exorcisms in public. Most notable of these is Emmanuel Milingo, born in 1930 in the country now known as Zambia, and consecrated in 1969 as Archbishop of Lusaka by Pope Paul VI.

As an Archbishop, Milingo's activities were unusual, for he spent far more time in conducting exorcisms than he did in administering his archdiocese and he also published a number of pamphlets on the subject of demons and witches. From these it is clear that he saw his archiepiscopal functions as largely concerned with expelling Ashtaroth and other evil spirits from the possessed and keeping the gates of hell firmly shut. Evil spirits, he warned, are to be dreaded more than witches. He wrote:

> The witches are merely human beings who . . . kill their own offspring . . . commit incest, torture their fellow human beings . . . The spirits . . . are stealing . . . from the hands of Christ . . . [Like witches they] kill, but in a different way. They forbid the patient to eat . . . foods.

Archbishop Milingo's preoccupations alarmed the Vatican and he was called to Rome where he was for a time confined to a monastery and underwent psychiatric investigations at the orders of the Pope.

Demon in denim

Archbishop Milingo was found to be completely sane and since then has acquired a sizeable European following, notably in Italy, where a belief in bewitchment and the powers of those supposedly possessed of the 'evil eye' is still surprisingly common.

In Italy the Archbishop's public exorcisms are carried out in the church of Santa Maria Adolorato, the only place in Rome at which he is permitted to officiate. These attract large congregations and a good deal of attention from journalists. One such journalist, who attended an exorcism in the autumn of 1986, described a service which seems to be fairly typical:

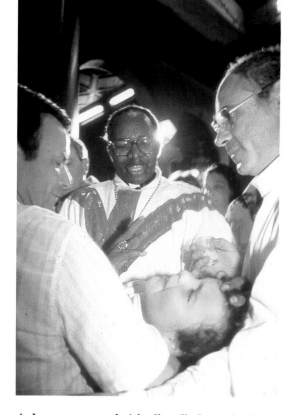

A demon-possessed girl, allegedly bewitched by a relative, screams and writhes as she awaits the administrations of Archbishop Milingo.

> The congregation included one woman who believed that her mother-in-law had put a spell on her, another who had been 'wasting away' as a result of bewitchment until the Archbishop exorcised her, another, clad in blue denim, who grunted like a pig, and yet another who writhed convulsively upon the floor.

The service, which incorporated a mass, lasted for over five hours, with the Archbishop continually calling out the names of demons – Lucifer, Nambroth, Bechet, Nabam and a host of others – and commanding them to depart from those they were afflicting.

At least some of those present seemed to benefit.

Archbishop Milingo – his sermons were concerned very largely with demonology and witchcraft.

SATAN AND THE CHARISMATICS

It is not only Catholics who are concerned with the activities of Satan at the present day and are convinced that diabolical possession is a reality. A number of Protestant groups, both inside and outside the major Churches, share the same beliefs and carry out exorcisms which, while different in form from those of Catholicism are intended to achieve the same results – the expulsion of demons from human bodies and the healing of Satan's victims.

Most of the groups in question are allied with what is usually called 'the charismatic movement'. The charismatics believe that the gifts of the Holy Spirit – healing, speaking in strange languages, and so on – which were given to the early Christians at the first Pentecost (Whitsun) are still available to the faithful at the present day. The charismatics therefore practise spiritual healing, enter trance states in which they are unconscious of everyday things and utter seemingly meaningless strings of syllables, and purport to 'cast out demons' by prayer.

There is no doubt that some of those who have been the recipients of charismatic exorcisms – mostly young people who have claimed to be obsessed or possessed by demons as a result of participating in sorcery, black magic or modern witchcraft – have benefited psychologically from their ministrations. There is also no doubt that a minority of charismatics have been gullible to the point of foolishness on the subjects of diabolism and black magic.

Servant of Lucifer

An example of this gullibility was provided in the spring of 1986 when a lengthy and costly trial revealed that an English trickster, a man with a long string of criminal convictions, mostly for minor offences, had relieved a number of wealthy and socially prominent Christians of a sum in the region of a quarter of a million pounds by pretending to be a leading servant of Lucifer.

The trickster, a man named Derry Mainwaring-Knight, originally approached the Rector of his Sussex parish asking for advice on money matters. Subsequently he became aware that the Rector was extremely interested in black magic, witchcraft and possession and proceeded to go into what the Rector looked upon as a genuine trance. During this trance Mainwaring-Knight spoke in a strange voice, believed by the Rector to be that of Lucifer, and behaved in other peculiar ways.

Over the next few weeks and months the Rector

Many of the charismatic Christians of the present day believe in an approaching 'reign of Antichrist' – a false prophet, probably an occultist, who for a time will bring the world under the rule of Lucifer.

heard from Mainwaring-Knight the supposed story of his life. He was the 'descendant of 33 generations of satanists'. His grandmother had offered him to Lucifer when he was still a child. At her instigation a devil worshipping surgeon had conducted an operation on Mainwaring-Knight's brain which enabled Satan to take it over at any time he wished.

A golden throne

Mainwaring-Knight had risen to almost the topmost rank of the satanic conspiracy to which his grandmother had admitted him but had now, so he said, 'found Christ' and wanted to destroy 'the Devil's Church'. He could not do so, however, until he had purchased various items of satanic regalia on which he had sworn oaths; such regalia included a set of mysterious keys, a sceptre, a chalice, and a golden throne which was situated, surrounded by water, in a London flat.

This extraordinary farrago was accepted as truth by the Rector, who so strongly believed it that he approached a number of wealthy Christians, amongst them the wife of Timothy Sainsbury, a minister in Mrs Thatcher's government, for help. After much prayer these good, but credulous, Christians contributed to raise the £250,000 required. It was spent, not on satanic regalia but on prostitutes, sports cars and similar fleshly delights.

Eventually Mainwaring-Knight received a long prison sentence for fraud, but, amazingly, some of his victims continued to believe in the truth of the story he had told.

From the point of view of charismatic Christianity Satan's treasures are those souls he has stolen, by sorcery and other sins, from God.

A North London clergyman, a strong believer in the reality of demonic possession, endeavouring to exorcize a young woman whose mind, so it was thought, had been influenced by Satan.

In spite of the somewhat curious costumes once worn by Anton La Vey, founder of the Church of Satan, he has written books which are clearly the product of a penetrating intellect.

Many of the unhappy people who approach both Catholic priests and groups of charismatic Christians for their help claim that they are either persecuted by demons or possessed by devils. When asked to suggest a reason, or reasons, for hell's particular interest they tend to admit that they have dabbled in black magic or have participated in witchcraft rituals, or have been members of satanic societies which allegedly worship the Devil.

The stories told by those who claim to have been involved in satanism tend to bear an uncanny resemblance to one another. They were, they say, participants in ceremonies involving the sacrifice of animals, perverted sexuality, urine drinking and other unpleasant practices. One could draw the conclusion that either there are a very large number of groups engaging in similar perverted practices or that many mentally disturbed individuals share the same fantasies.

On the whole both possibilities seem fairly unlikely. It is more probable that some of those who ask for the help of Christians in dealing with the attacks of demons are entirely deluded or fraudulent but that others have become mentally afflicted – or even authentically possessed – as a result of participating in the rites of satanic, or pseudo-satanic, groupings.

A hellish spice

There is a certain amount of evidence that such groupings do actually exist, although it seems likely that their membership is far smaller, and their activities less iniquitous, than Christians concerned with occultism tend to believe.

There may even be some self-styled groups of diabolists whose activities are, save from a strictly theological point of view, totally innocent. Some years ago I met the leaders of one such 'satanic' group and came to the conclusion that none of their activities were particularly blameworthy and that they called themselves satanists for no better reason than that it gave them the publicity they desired.

Other groups have motives for their activities which stem from a perverted eroticism. A certain amount of blasphemy is employed in order to give a hellish spice to pursuits which are very little different from those of suburban 'swingers' – lechery rather than Lucifer worship is predominant.

Notwithstanding these provisos it cannot be denied that there have been, and probably still are, black magical groups whose doings have been evil in the extreme. The Manson 'family', responsible for a number of sadistic murders, including that of Sharon Tate, provides the best example of such a group in our own times.

Church of Satan

The Manson gang were described as 'kooks and creeps out of their minds on drugs' by Anton La Vey, who founded the California-based Church of Satan in the 1960s and, strangely, does not seem to believe in the personal existence of the Devil. For La Vey satanism is not devil worship but 'the worship of life' and, as such,

Milton, it has been claimed, unwittingly made Satan the hero of his epic poem, *Paradise Lost*. Certainly this is how he is discerned by contemporary satanists, who see him as the arch-rebel and individualist.

Like many other practitioners of magic, both black and white, Anton La Vey cluttered his home with skulls and the impedimenta traditionally associated with sorcery.

'concerned with the fullest gratification of the ego on this plane of existence'.

In spite of this statement, which makes it sound as though La Vey's diabolism was never more than an assertion of the pleasures of the senses, there is no doubt that he and his numerous followers – at one time the membership of the Church of Satan was estimated at approaching 25,000 – are deeply involved in the occult, of which he has a wide ranging knowledge.

Nor is there any doubt that La Vey has frequently celebrated the Black Mass on the bodies of nude women – indeed, he has been filmed doing so. La Vey's Black Masses, however, are lacking in the horror of the authentic rite, and the 'human sacrifices' which are incorporated in them are no more than the solemn spanking of volunteer victims. Amusingly enough the 'sacrifice', unless a masochist, is allowed to wear heavily padded trousers . . .

Nevertheless, the Church and groups derived from it are regarded with horror by a good many Christians.

MODERN WITCHCRAFT

At the present day a very large number of men and women in North America and Europe consider themselves to be witches. That is to say, they believe themselves to be practising an ancient fertility religion based on the worship of a great Mother Goddess and a Horned God. Further, they affirm that at least some members of their cult, often referred to as 'the craft', possess a knowledge of ancient magical techniques which can be used for good or ill, for blessing or cursing.

It is possible that the origins of the modern witch cult go far back into the past, that an ancient faith has survived into the present day. It has to be admitted, however, that very few people in the western world were aware of the existence of modern witchcraft until 1954, the year in which Gerald Gardner, a retired civil servant, published his book *Witchcraft Today*.

The Book of Shadows

At some time in the late 1930s Gardner was admitted to a witchcraft group operating in southern England and subsequently he came into contact, so he said, with a number of similar groups. Gardner's book was a guarded revelation of the beliefs and practices of the members of these groups, 'covens'. The words he quoted from one coven member summarized their faith:

Ours is a religion of love, pleasure and excitement . . . we worship the divine spirit of Creation . . . without which the world would perish. To us it is the most sacred and holy mystery . . . Such rites are done in a holy and reverent way.

Mr Alec Sanders, once known as 'King of the Witches', conducts a pagan wedding ceremony. The crowns worn by the happy couple are based on those described in the *grimoire* known as *Abramelin*.

A coven of the contemporary witch cult celebrates a fire festival – unlike many other groups of this sort they are eschewing being 'sky clad', as nudity is referred to.

This seems to indicate that the rites of the groups with which Gardner was in contact were in some way concerned with human sexuality. This surmise is confirmed by some parts of *The Book of Shadows*, a sort of witchcraft instructional manual which Gardner circulated in manuscript amongst those he himself initiated into the cult. It is possible that *The Book of Shadows*, which is now available in printed form, is a modern derivation of a genuinely ancient occult text. If so it was greatly altered and added to by some 20th-century witch, for it contains a folksy 'witch chant' which is an adaptation of a poem by Rudyard Kipling, extracts from a 19th-century book on Italian witchcraft, and some passages strongly reminiscent of the writings of Aleister Crowley.

The new pagans

Witchcraft Today attracted a surprisingly wide readership and following its publication there was a mushroom growth of modern witchcraft. Some of this was directly derived from Gerald Gardner and those he had initiated into the cult by rites, allegedly traditional, involving nudity, very mild scourging and a certain amount of occult ceremony. In view of some of the lurid and unpleasant publicity which some newspapers gave to Gardner's activities it is worth adding that there is no reliable evidence that the initiations he conducted were in any way obscene or perverted.

Other groups devoted to modern witchcraft came into existence quite independently of Gardner, those who led them claiming to have been initiated into the craft by elderly relatives. The most active of these non-Gardnerian witches was Mr Alec Sanders who, in the late 1960s, inducted a large number of his occult pupils into the cult and whose followers became termed 'Alexandrian witches'.

Few groups now practise 'pure' witchcraft in either its Gardnerian or Alexandrian versions, but what is sometimes called 'the new paganism' has evolved from it. These new pagans practise with great sincerity, and with benefit to many, a magical and religious system based on the worship of the old gods, the personified male and female principles of nature.

A certain cinematic influence can be discerned in this goat's head, once employed by a leading member of a contemporary witch cult in dramatic occult ceremonies.

INNER DEMONS

Many people who would not look upon themselves as being particularly interested in demonology, witchcraft or black magic get great pleasure from reading supernatural fiction. The 'ghost stories' of M.R. James, many of which are concerned with witchcraft and black magic, for example.

Most of us have our own 'inner demons', a desire to be pleasantly frightened, which is fed by fiction, cinema and even music which have been influenced by traditional occult beliefs.

The cinema, perhaps the only completely new art form to develop in the 1,500 years or so preceding the invention of the computer and the visual experimentation which it has made possible, has brought the themes of witchcraft, demonic possession and black magic into the consciousness of millions.

The earliest effective use of such a theme was provided by *The Student of Prague*, made in 1913 by the Danish director Stellan Rye and, in essence, a cinematic presentation of the story of Faust.

In the following year the film's star, Paul Wegener, directed *The Golem*, a film which was based on the legendary story of how in the 16th century a wonder working Rabbi magically created a *golem*, a body without a soul, from mud. In Wegener's retelling of the story a 'human interest' was given to the tale by making the golem fall in love with its creator's daughter, become insanely violent when rejected by her, and finally be destroyed by a fall from a tower.

Frankenstein and Dracula

Both these films were, of course, European and, in fact, Hollywood showed little interest in supernatural themes until the commercial success of *Frankenstein* and *Dracula*, both released in 1931. While these films came from a Hollywood studio it is significant that they strongly reflected European influences. The plot of *Frankenstein* owed quite as much to *The Golem* as it did to Mary Shelley's novel and while *Dracula* followed Bram Stoker's plot it was filmed by a brilliantly innovative German cameraman, Karl Freund, and had a Bulgarian star in Bela Lugosi.

At the same time as *Dracula* was being made in Hollywood the Danish director Carl Dreyer was making a vampire film based on Sheridan Le Fanu's short novel *Carmilla*. The instructions he gave to his cameraman admirably described the transformation of consciousness, the altered perception of reality, which in the best films devoted to supernatural themes awake the inner demons within the minds of the audience. He said:

Imagine we are sitting in an ordinary room. Suddenly we are told there is a corpse behind the door. In an instant the room we are sitting in is completely altered, everything in it has taken on another level . . . This is because we have changed . . . This is the effect I want to get.

Nosferatu, a 1970s' remake of the classic German vampire film of the 1920s, is almost unique in its pessimism, its finale being the triumph of evil.

The Devil's child

Carmilla has Lesbian undertones, of which its author may well have been unconscious, and a great many vampire films of the last 25 years contain similar elements, sometimes conveyed fairly explicitly. This was particularly so in the case of many of the successful Hammer films, which also tended to put a perhaps undue emphasis on realistically bloody effects. While such films were triumphs of cinematic technique many feel that they failed to achieve the archetypal power of the classic Bela Lugosi's *Dracula*.

The best supernatural film of the last 20 years or so was perhaps Polanski's *Rosemary's Baby* (1968), a film in which satanist leader Anton La Vey played the part of the Devil. The film, a treatment of the ancient theme of the *incubus* (see page 56) showed that it is possible to combine technical brilliance with the consciousness alteration which was the aim of Carl Dreyer.

Many of Willy Dixon's lyrics contained references to 'hexes', witchcraft, and magical potions, notably those believed to induce sexual attraction or to be possessed of aphrodisiac qualities.

In the southern USA, notably in Louisiana, a curious witchcraft and folk magic evolved from a blend of African religious and magical beliefs with European sorcery and demonology as expressed in degenerate occult texts such as *The Fifth And Sixth Book Of Moses*, a book of spells which seems to have derived from a 17th-century German text.

This type of witchcraft, and the beliefs in demons and devils associated wih it, was sometimes reflected in the lyrics of the Blues, the bitter and beautiful music of black America from which Rock has evolved.

The Blues, rural and urban, were always disliked by some black Americans, who saw them as being literally devilish—Satan's response to gospel music. Some Blues musicians were offended by the accusation that they were doing the Devil's work when they sang of the experiences of poverty, sexuality and alcoholism which they had themselves undergone. Others almost gloried in it. Thus Blues singer William Bunch, professionally known as 'Peetie Wheatstraw', boasted of knowing Satan and called himself 'The Devil's Son-in-Law and High Sheriff of Hell'.

High John the Conqueror

Wheatstraw may well have adopted his claim to be on good terms with the Devil to annoy the pious, and may not have even believed in the existence of Satan. This last was not, however, true of the talented guitarist and singer Robert Johnson who believed that Satan was ever-active in the modern world, and out to get him personally, and sang convincingly of the 'Hell Hound on my Trail'.

The urban Rhythm and Blues tradition which grew up in the black ghettoes of Chicago and other northern cities in the 20 years or so following the great stockmarket crash of 1929 contained elements which demonstrated the survival of a belief in devils, witchcraft and black magic.

Thus many of the songs of Chicago musician Willy Dixon, recorded by both himself and such Rhythm and Blues stars as Chuck Berry and Muddy Waters, contain specific references to spells, witchcraft, and magic potions and herbs, notably a root referred to as 'High John the Conqueror', renowned for its supposedly aphrodisiac qualities.

The early 1970s' concerts of Dr John the Night Tripper strongly reflected the influence of what has been called 'Louisiana swamp magic'.

Screamin' Jay Hawkins gave an impressive 'magical' performance – but most serious students of the occult who saw him in action felt that it was more vaudeville than voodoo.

The Night Tripper

The use of High John originated amongst the black practitioners of Louisiana's own brand of witchcraft and folk magic. Oddly, however, the musician who has most frequently referred to it in his lyrics, which also mention such mysterious substances as 'goofer powder' and 'drawing dust', is white – a one time session musician named Malcolm Rebennack who became known as Dr John the Night Tripper. Dr John's stage performances of the early 1970s were suggestive of authentic occult rites and some believe he seriously thought of himself as a magician; certainly many of those who watched them felt that they had attended a gathering more akin to a voodoo ceremony than to a musical performance.

The 'goofer dust' referred to in Dr John's lyrics is earth taken from a freshly dug grave and is used in Louisiana witchcraft in order to kill or injure an enemy. 'Drawing powder' is used for more innocent types of spells. It consists of powdered lodestone, a natural magnetic ore, or magnetized iron filings and has been subjected to magical techniques which are believed to have imbued it with the power of attracting love, money, power or general good fortune to its owner.

Whether Dr John took himself altogether seriously in his adopted role of voodoo magician is uncertain, nor is it known to what extent he shared the beliefs of which he sang – but it is undoubted that they provided the structural framework for the remarkable albums which he recorded.

Just as the lyrics of rural and urban Blues sometimes reflected beliefs associated with the folk magic of Louisiana so Rock, child of the Blues, has reflected not only traditional magical lore but both the innocent and sinister aspects of the current occult revival.

Traditional magical beliefs held some attraction for both Bob Marley and Jimi Hendrix, and they were particularly impressed by Akonidi Hini, a Ghanaian occultist and healer who has sometimes been inaccurately referred to as 'the High Priestess of Voodoo'. Akonidi believed that the magical ceremonies she carried out in her temple were responsible for Hendrix's commercial success and it is interesting to note that he dedicated his 'Voodoo Chile' to her.

Akonidi still takes an interest in all types of black music and its performers – in 1982, for example, she undertook a 'three day spiritual fast' to bless Eddie Grant's UK chart-topping single 'I Don't Wanna Dance'.

A Demented Hamlet

Some Rock musicians have used a satanic/black magical presentation of their material for its theatrical value and it cannot be assumed that an expressed concern with the Devil, hell and ritual magic shows any real

Blue Oyster Cult, who use the alchemical symbol for lead as their insignia, sing complex lyrics centred around strange rites similar to those described in the sinister occult stories of H.P. Lovecraft.

This simulated human sacrifice, performed on stage by the Californian group Black Widow, indicated a strong sense of theatre rather than active involvement in black magic and witchcraft.

occult commitment. It is difficult, for example, to believe in the total sincerity of Screamin' Jay Hawkins who in the early 1970s was accustomed to perform 'I Put A Spell On You' while juggling with a skull like a demented Hamlet.

On the other hand there is no good reason to doubt the sincerity of the lyrics of the Keith Richard/Mick Jagger 'Sympathy for the Devil', recorded in 1968, which presented Satan as the eternal rebel and anarchist and, as such, the archetype of the streetwise Rock devotee.

'Sympathy for the Devil' has been referred to as satanic Rock, a term which could more appropriately be applied to the album 'Sacrifice' recorded by the Californian group Black Widow in 1970.

The lyrics of the songs recorded on this album, which include 'Come to the Sabbat', 'Attack of the Demon', and 'Conjuration', abound with references to demons, witchcraft and ritual magic. There are many allusions to 'the secret art', Satan, Ashtaroth and so on. These have led some fundamentalist Christians to believe that the album provides an excellent example of how Satan uses Rock to convert people to devil worship.

This may be so. On the other hand it may be that, as was suggested by the journalist Paul Green some years ago, the album is an example of, not diabolism, but diabolically bad taste.

Black Sabbath

The tracks recorded in the early 1970s by the British heavy metal group Black Sabbath also aroused worries amongst convinced Christians. The group's performances, both live and recorded, displayed what seemed to be a genuine and chilling concern with Satan and devil worship.

Each concert began with what seemed to be an authentic magical ceremony, probably derived from one of the occult textbooks known as the *grimoires*, which most of the audience seem to have found both eerie and, on occasion, over long. This preliminary rite was considered so authentic by a prominent member of the modern witch cult that he approached the group to warn them that 'they were in danger of raising forces beyond their control'.

It is possible that some members of the group took this warning seriously, for subsequently the group played down the satanic aspects of its performances and it was even claimed that its concern with Satan worship was to *warn* people against it.

There are no well-known Rock groups concerned with satanism – but the early albums of Black Widow and Black Sabbath are still played by admirers, satanic and otherwise.

Black Sabbath, a Heavy Metal group whose early performances were remarkably eerie, toned down their presentations after a leading member of the modern witch cult warned them that they were raising 'forces beyond their control'.

At least one menber of the group Killing Joke whose lead singer is depicted here, believed so strongly in occult prophecy that he retired for a time to Iceland to avoid a catastrophe he believed to be imminent.

The witches in Shakespeare's *Macbeth* supernaturally produce a vision of the future rulers of both Scotland and England.

The nightmare supernatural imaginations of Poe, which probably owed something to his experimentation with laudanum – opium infused in brandy – were given visual form in this illustration by Arthur Rackham.

Since Shakespeare wrote *Macbeth* almost 300 years ago supernatural themes concerned with black magic, demonology and witchcraft have provided the constructional framework of a large number of plays, novels and short stories.

Many of these are now rightly forgotten. Others are still readable with enjoyment at the present day. One, Goethe's *Faust*, is a masterpiece which has an abiding importance which transcends its theme and speaks to us of the human condition as clearly – perhaps even more clearly – at the present day as it did when it was first published.

Shakespeare and Goethe were spiritual and literary giants, but there have been many other writers who have used supernatural themes in works of genuine literary value – for example Maupassant, Henry James, Sheridan Le Fanu and M.R. James.

Suspension of disbelief

The first two of these were men of undoubted genius, but neither was greatly concerned with black magic, demonology and witchcraft. Henry James' *Turn of the Screw* was an example, perhaps the only example, of the classic ghost story raised to the dignity of an art form. And Maupassant's genuinely chilling supernatural stories reflect the fears and delusions of a brain poisoned by the toxins of syphilis, a mind poised on the brink of madness, rather than any profound acquaintance with the lore of magic and demonology.

The short stories of Le Fanu and M.R. James display a more intimate knowledge of occult traditions, which the former had acquired through his study of the writings of the 18th-century mystic Emmanuel

Swedenborg, the latter through his scholarly researches into medieval and Renaissance manuscripts.

Both succeeded in achieving what M.R. James thought should be the main object of a writer handling supernatural themes, the production of a 'willing suspension of disbelief' in the reader. In other words, while such a story is being read the man or woman reading it, even if an utter sceptic, should be induced to believe, for the time being, in ghosts, witches and demons.

Le Fanu is still enormously readable, but the master of the literary 'ghost' story was M.R. James; the word 'ghost' has been put in inverted commas because many of James's stories are really concerned with black magic and demons rather than the spirits of the dead.

Demon guardian

Thus, for example, in *The Treasure of Abbot Thomas* an antiquary who has discovered the site of a 16th-century treasure is prevented from retrieving it by the demon guardian in whose care the sorcerous Abbot had placed it. Similarly *The Ash Tree* is concerned with a number of unpleasant deaths – the corpses are found so bloated and distorted that their features are recognized only with difficulty – resulting from witchcraft, while *Count Magnus* is a story of black magic, the count having been a sorcerer who had made 'the black pilgrimage', whatever that may have been.

Although M.R. James expressed an opinion that too much occult theory was deleterious to tales of the supernatural, pointing to the writings of Algernon Blackwood as examples of this fault, there seems some

In '*Oh, Whistle And I'll Come to You*' M.R. James' protagonist, an academic suffering from nervous strain, was attacked by a demon guardian which used bed sheets to give itself physical form.

likelihood that he had a knowledge of the activities of one or two magicians of his own time. This is strongly suggested by his story *Casting the Runes* which not only describes a demonic death spell of a type certainly being experimented with at the time the tale was written, but has a villain combining 'much learning with little scholarship' who bears a passing resemblance to MacGregor Mathers as he might have been portrayed by an orthodox Christian. Whether or not this was the case there is no doubt that, as a writer, James remains a magician with the power of evoking our inner demons.

Many of the so-called ghost stories of M.R. James are in reality tales of black magic, witchcraft and traffic with demons. Notable amongst the latter group is that illustrated here, *Canon Alberic's Scrapbook*.

Not surprisingly much of the most effective of this fiction has been written by people who were at one time or another members of the magical secret societies derived from the activities and teachings of MacGregor Mathers (see page 122). Thus in the novels *Moonchild* and *The Devil's Mistress*, written by, respectively, Aleister Crowley and Brodie Innes, there were given complex magical interpretations of witchcraft and its connections with repressed sexuality and the Great God Pan, identified by both writers with the Devil of Christian belief.

The novelist Brodie Innes, like Dion Fortune, derived much of his occult philosophy from prolonged brooding and meditation on MacGregor Mathers' interpretation of the tarot trumps. Ideas connected with this card influenced his novel *The Devil's Mistress*.

Dion Fortune, the magician whose novels were largely concerned with the esoteric aspects of human sexuality, saw the White Eagle and the Green Lion depicted in this tarot card as symbols of male/female polarity.

Since the final decade of the last century a certain amount of supernatural fiction has been written by men and women whose aim has been the *deliberate* arousal of the inner demons which lurk beneath the level of the conscious mind. These authors have themselves been practising magicians or witches and have used their novels and short stories as a means of, firstly, conveying occult teachings and, secondly, bringing their readers into a state of mind in which they more easily come into contact with what can either be called 'supernatural forces' or, if one likes to use the terminology of the psychologist C.G. Jung, 'archetypes present in the Collective Unconscious'.

The wine of the sabbath

Both of these writers also dealt with what has been called 'human atavism'. By this is meant the reversion of mind, or even matter, to earlier evolutionary forms, a concept probably derived from Mathers' interpretations of the nature of Lilith (see page 95) and other demons.

Another author who wrote of these primitive, atavistic aspects of witchcraft and black magic was Arthur Machen, also at one time an initiate of Mathers' magical order.

Machen first dealt with magical atavism in his short novel *The Great God Pan*, first published in 1894 and described by a reviewer in the *Manchester Guardian* as 'the most acutely and intentionally disagreeable we have yet seen in English'.

In episodic form the novel recounts the life of Helen Vaughan, a literal child of Pan, whose inherited powers of witchery enable her to destroy, both morally and physically, all those with whom she comes into a close relationship. Her destructive career ends with her suicide and the atavistic reversion of her body to protoplasmic slime.

Machen returned to the theme of atavism in his *Novel of the White Powder*, which recounts the story of a young man who takes what he believes is a harmless tonic but is in reality the Wine of the Sabbath, a sinister brew drunk by witches. The *Vinum Sabbati* first destroys him morally and then physically – his body deliquescing into a loathsome black ichor.

The Black Isis

The most deliberate attempts to use fiction as an occult tool were made by Dion Fortune (1890–1946), another student of the magical system formulated by MacGregor Mathers.

Her first really successful occult novels were *Goatfoot God* and *Winged Bull* both published in the 1930s. The first told the story of a repressed man who found psychic salvation through magic, the remembrance of a previous incarnation in which he had been an even more repressed monk, and marriage. The second concerned a magical operation designed to unify the physical and spiritual aspects of human sexuality.

Her most successful novels, in both the literary and magical aspects were *Sea Priestess* (1938) and its posthumously published sequel *Moon Magic*. Both these books expressed Dion Fortune's beliefs that modern mankind has lost touch with the Black Isis, the primordial feminine, and that every woman must practise a type of magic by which she becomes a priestess of this goddess.

These books, still in print, continue to exert an influence on present day magicians and witches.

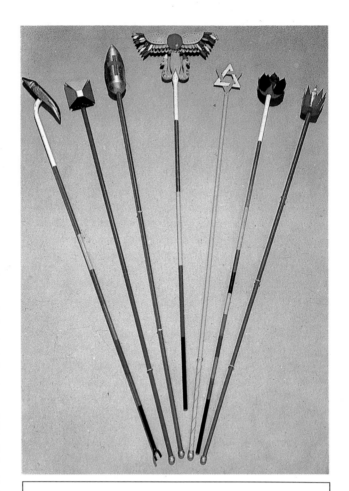

Most of the magicians who wrote novels in which occult teachings were conveyed under the guise of fiction, amongst them Dion Fortune and Brodie Innes, had trained in the secret Order in which wands identical to these were employed in ritual workings (see also above).

The late Seabury Quinn, a leading American mortician – for a time he edited the improbably named trade journal *Casket and Sunnyside* – once visited, in totally innocent circumstances, a New Orleans brothel. He was immediately surrounded by all the girls who worked there, not because they considered him a potential client, but because they were all enthusiastic admirers of the black magic and witchcraft stories he regularly wrote for the magazine *Weird Tales*.

During the life of *Weird Tales* (1922–54) Seabury Quinn was its most popular author, having over 90 stories published, 33 of which were the subjects of cover illustrations. At the present day the plots of most of them seem fairly predictable, but when they were first printed they were better received by the magazine's readership than were stories by authors such as M.R. James. The very crudity of Quinn's handling of occult

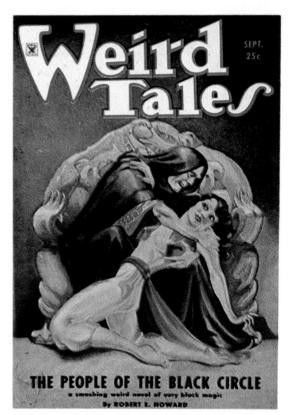

THE PEOPLE OF THE BLACK CIRCLE
a smashing weird novel of very black magic
By ROBERT E. HOWARD

Although they usually bore little relationship to the stories they illustrated Margaret Brundage's covers were extremely popular with the readers of *Weird Tales* – perhaps because they almost invariably featured a scantily clad girl.

The ancient Faust theme – human beings controlled by the lords of hell – was a recurring element in the occult pulp fiction of the period 1920–1950.

themes appealed to *something* in the collective psyche of Americans of that period.

While Quinn was the most commercially successful of the many new writers who reached a wide readership through *Weird Tales* he was probably the one who is less remembered and reprinted than all the others – Clark Ashton Smith, Robert E. Howard, Robert Bloch and, above all, H.P. Lovecraft (1890–1937).

Power and malignancy

Lovecraft has been the most influential of these, for he has not only had many imitators but, strangely, has received a great deal of attention from some occultists who have chosen to take his fiction as representing an underlying reality of which most people are unaware.

The essential features of the imaginary mythology

H.P. Lovecraft's *Through the Gates of the Silver Key* was contained in this issue of *Weird Tales* – but it was a novelette by the now forgotten Arlton Eadie which was featured on the cover.

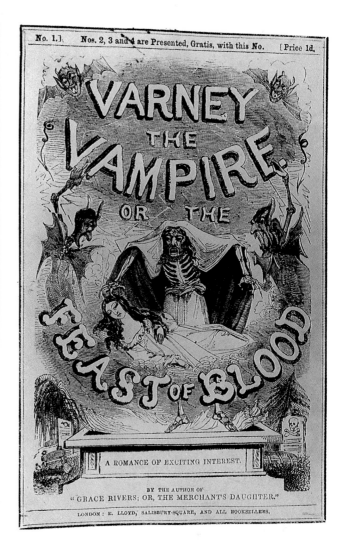

Varney the Vampire, an interminable supernatural story issued in weekly parts (price one penny) by an early Victorian publisher, was a fore-runner of the supernatural pulp fiction of the 1930s.

which provided the structural framework of the fiction which Lovecraft wrote in his maturity are as follows. Firstly, that humanity is ignorant of the real nature of the universe – there are other dimensions of space which are full of beings of terrifying power and malignancy. Secondly, that earth was once ruled by some of these beings, the Great Old Ones, who somehow or other lost control of it but are perpetually endeavouring to regain their lost dominion. And, finally, that all over the world exist individuals and groups who have chosen to ally themselves with the Great Old Ones.

In essence those three points are no more than restatements in a different terminology of the ideology of the demonologists of the Middle Ages and the Renaissance. The 'other dimensions of space' and the creatures who dwell there are hell and its denizens; the Great Old Ones are Lucifer and his angels; their human allies are witches and black magicians.

A natural magician

From his correspondence it is clear that on a conscious level Lovecraft did not believe a word of the imaginary mythology that is outlined above; he was not in any sense a religious man.

Nevertheless from the first publication of his stories in *Weird Tales* and other pulps – so called because publications of this sort were printed on paper made from the cheapest grade of wood pulp – there have been occultists who have devoted great attention to them and have argued that Lovecraft was a 'natural magician' who had, through dreams and archetypal material rising up from the depths of the unconscious, come into contact with supernatural forces and acquired a knowledge of cosmic realities. Thus, for example, more than one follower of Aleister Crowley has argued for a correspondence between elements in Lovecraft's mythology and Crowley's magic.

Some have gone further and been prepared to *worship* Lovecraft's demons, the Great Old Ones, using for this purpose an elaborate ritual composed in their honour by Anton La Vey, founder of the Church of Satan and an admirer of Lovecraft. In such ways Lovecraft's inner demons have acquired a certain reality.

DEMONS OF THE LAST DAYS

The earliest Christians were all convinced that the end of the world was imminent. They were sure that those who had known Jesus in the flesh would live to see him return to earth, raise to life all those who had died since the Creation, and give the final judgement on each and every human being.

As the decades and the centuries rolled by most Christians no longer thought that the Second Coming of Christ would take place in their own lifetimes. They firmly believed, of course, in the eventual return of Christ to earth in order to judge the living and the dead, but they thought it possible that these events might not come to pass for hundreds or thousands of years.

There have always, however, been small and passionately sincere groups of Christians who have believed that the end of all things is at hand. They have interpreted the events of their own lifetimes – wars, plagues, famines, political and social upheavals – as indications of an approaching finality. On the basis of complex numerical calculations involving symbolic interpretation of some of the books of the Bible, notably *Daniel* and *Revelations*, some of these groups have even announced not just the date but the time of the expected Second Coming. Thus, for example, Walter Miller, a Baptist preacher in upstate New York first announced the event for a particular day and probable time in March 1843; then for a date six months later; and finally for a date in 1844. In spite of these three bitter disappointments – some of Miller's followers had clad themselves in white clothes and climbed

Many 'born-again' Christians, particularly in the USA, believe that the Second Coming of Christ, the resurrection of the dead, and the final judgement are imminent.

It is believed that the expected appearance of the 'Four Horsemen of the Apocalypse', foretold in the final book of the New Testament, will signify the beginning of the events ending in the Second Coming.

high hills in order to get a good view of the Second Coming – the new worldwide Seventh Day Adventist Church has grown out of Millerism.

Born again Christians

At the present day belief in the imminent end of the world and the Second Coming is more widespread amongst Christians than at any time since the first century AD. For not only do large organizations which are, in a sense, outside mainstream Christianity – the Jehovah's Witnesses for example – believe that the end is nigh, but similar beliefs are entertained by a very large number of those 'born again' Christians who are active in every Church in the western world, but particularly so in the United States of America.

Very shortly, so it is asserted, events prophesied in the distant past will come about. The world will be swept by great plagues and Satan will make his last attempts to control humanity, many of whom will follow 'the Beast 666' and take up arms against Christ and his followers in the Battle of Armageddon.

Mark of the Beast

Those who hold such beliefs view the occult revival which has taken place over the last century or so, and its influence on cinema, music and other art forms as evidence of the coming upheavals and catastrophes. The devotees of modern witchcraft, Satanism and all forms of occultism will be, so it is said, the shock troops of Satan in his final struggle against the forces of good. They will, of course, be defeated – the apocalypse, it is pointed out, specifically informs us that sorcerers will be cast into everlasting fire.

Prior to this interesting event there will be a brief period when Satan and his sorcerers will seem to have triumphed. Those of us who have not received 'the mark of the Beast' will find ourselves unable to buy food because cash will no longer be of any value and credit cards will only be acceptable from those who worship the Beast.

If all this proves correct we shall shortly see the four horsemen of the Apocalypse – pestilence, war, famine and death – the demons of finality.

Figures in italics refer to captions

FURTHER READING

Those who would like to know more of witchcraft and magic, both past and present, will find it useful to read one or more of the following.

Cavendish, Richard	*The Magical Arts*	Arkana, London, 1984
Cavendish, Richard	*The Powers of Evil*	Routledge, London, 1975
Cohn, Norman	*Europe's Inner Demons*	Sussex Univ. Press, 1975
d'Arch Smith, Timothy	*The Books of The Beast*	Aquarian, Wellingborough, 1986
King, Francis	*Magic – The Western Tradition*	Thames & Hudson, London, 1975
Mathers, S.L. MacGregor	*Astral Projection, Ritual Magic and Alchemy*	Aquarian, Wellingborough, 1987
Richardson, Alan	*Dancers to The Gods*	Aquarian, Wellingborough, 1985
Richardson, Alan	*Priestess*	Aquarian, Wellingborough, 1987
Robertson, Sandy	*Rock Magick*	Aquarian, Wellingborough, 1987
Skinner, Stephen	*Terrestrial Astrology*	Routledge, London, 1980

Acknowledgments of Photographs and Paintings

The Publishers would like to thank the following contributors to the book. Whilst every effort has been made to trace all present copyright holders of this material, whether companies or individuals, any unintentional omission is hereby apologized for in advance, and we should of course be pleased to correct any errors in acknowledgments in any future edition of this book.

Chapter openers: *Page 10:* Amenophis offers libation to Amun from Deir el Bahari. HGPL (Cairo Museum). *Page 32:* Witches at work by Hans Baldung Grün. BBC Hulton Picture Library. *Page 44:* The Witches Sabbat on the Brocken. Aldus Archive/BPCC (The Douce Collection, Bodleian Library, Oxford). *Page 70:* The Four Sorcerers by Albrecht Dürer. HGPL (British Museum, London). *Page 90:* Asmodeus the destroyer demon, from Collin de Plancy. Dictionnaire Infernal. HGPL. *Page 106:* Reign of Antichrist, 15th-century engraving. Pat Hodgson Library. *Page 120:* Tarot card designed by Freda Harris for Aleister Crowley. Michael Holford. *Page 140:* The Omen, directed by Richard Donner, 20th Century Fox. The Kobal Collection.

Aldus Archive/BPCC: 23 bottom (Collection Arna Magnaen, Denmark), 29 bottom (Bodleian Library, Oxford), 43 top & bottom, 44 (Bodleian Library, Oxford), 46 bottom, 53 left, 59 top, 82 (Kunsthaus Zurich, on loan from the G. Keller-Foundation, Bern), 94 *The Sefiroth by Dawson Godfrey,* 96, 102 top, 103 bottom (Ashmolean Museum, Oxford), 121, 122, 124, 130 top (Caroline Legerman), 135 top *The Treasures of Satan by Jean Delville* (Musées Royaux des Beaux-Arts, Brussels), 139, 154; BBC Hulton Picture Library: 32, 34, 37 top, 40 bottom, 49 bottom, 51 top, 56 top, 63 bottom, 80 bottom, 83 bottom, 86, 100 right, 105, 123 top & bottom, 125 top & bottom, 126 top & bottom; Bridgeman Art Library: 15 *The Gardens of Earthly Delights (right panel) by Hieronymus Bosch* (Prado Museum, Madrid), 47 *La Lampara del Diablo from El Hechizado por Fuerza by Francisco de Goya* (National Gallery, London), 53 *The Love Potion by Evelyn De Morgan* (The De Morgan Foundation, London), 62 *The Witch by Sir John Gilbert* (Guildhall Art Gallery, London), 69 *The Fairy Feller's Master-Stroke by Richard Dadd* (The Tate Gallery, London), 99 *The Cathedral Scene from Faust, Margaret tormented by Evil Spirits by F.C. Cowper* (Private Collection), 117 top *Woman on a Rocking Horse by Félicien Rops* (Reproduced by courtesy of the Trustees of the British Museum), 137 bottom *Satan, Sin and Death by William Blake* (Henry E. Huntingdon Library & Art Gallery, San Marino), 146 left *Macbeth by Theodore Chassériau* (Musée des Beaux Arts, Valenciennes/Giraudon), 152 *The Last Judgement by Stephan Lochner* (Wallraf-Richartz Museum, Cologne), 153 top *The Riders of the Apocalypse by Vasco Taskovski* (Imperial War Museum, London); 'Britain on View' (BTA/ETB): 112; The British Library, London: 29 top, 77 bottom, 92 left, 100 left, 118 top; Camera Press: 83 top (photo Sid Ross), 135 bottom (photo Colin Davey), 140; Jean-Loup Charmet: 26 top (Bibliothèque Nationale, Paris), 35 top (Bibliothèque Nationale, Paris), 36 (Bibliothèque Nationale, Paris), 55 bottom (Bibliothèque Nationale, Paris), 59 bottom, 60 top (Bibliothèque des Arts Décoratifs, Paris), 72 top (Bibliothèque Nationale, Paris), 87 left (Bibliothèque Nationale, Paris), 97 top (Bibliothèque Nationale, Paris), 107, 108, 130 bottom *Voodoo Dancing round a Pole by Rose-Marie Desruisseaux* (Haitian Embassy, France); Daily Telegraph Colour Library: 136, 137 top (photos Alexander Low); Courtesy of The Essex Institute, Salem, MA: 84, 85 top; E.T. Archive: 17 top *Cerberus by William Blake* (Tate Gallery, London), 20 *S. Zeno Exorcising the Daughter of the Emperor Gallienus. Pesellino. Florentine School* (The National Gallery, London), 37 *The Incantation by Frans Francken* (Victoria & Albert Museum, London), 105 top; Werner Forman Archive/Reproduced by courtesy of the Trustees of the British Museum: 102 bottom, 103 top; Fortean Picture Library/Janet & Colin Bord: 64 bottom; John Freeman & Co/Fotomas Index: 25, 35, 39 top, 39 bottom, 51 bottom, 76, 77 top, 81, 88 left; Raymond Galbraith: 128, 129 bottom; Giraudon: 12, 28 bottom *Conjuro by Francisco de Goya* (Lazaro Galdeano Museum, Madrid), 33 *The Sabbat by Francisco de Goya* (Lazaro Galdeano Museum, Madrid), 38 *The Witches' Sabbat by Francisco de Goya* (Prado Museum, Madrid), 45 *Mirror of Human Salvation. The Temptation of Christ. Daniel faces Beland a dragon. Flemish 15th-century manuscript* (Musée Condé, Chantilly); Robert Harding Picture Library: 129 top, 131, 134 *Lucifer and attendant devils from The Douce Collection* (The Bodleian Library, Oxford); HGPL: 11, 14 *The Fallen Angels entering Pandemonium from Paradise Lost Bk.1 by John Martin* (The Tate Gallery, London), 15 top *Satan Addressing the Fallen Angels by William Blake* (Victoria & Albert Museum, London), 16 *Hecate by William Blake* (Victoria & Albert Museum, London), 17 (British Museum, London), 18 (British Museum, London), 19 (British Museum, London), 23 top, 24 *The Wild Hunt by P.N. Arbo* (O. Vaering, Oslo), 42 (Hereford City Museum), 52 *Love's Enchantment,* Flemish painting (G. Reinhold, Leipzie-Mölkau), 67 (Wellcome Historical Medical Museum), 68 top & bottom, 80 top (Wellcome Historical Medical Museum), 87 right *The Nightmare by Henry Fuseli* (Goethe Museum, Frankfurt-am-Main), 90, 98 top, 114, 115 top & bottom, 117 bottom, 119 (Huysmans Society of Brussels), 146 right, 147 top & bottom; Pat Hodgson Library: 21 right (Dover Publications), 25 bottom (Dover Publications), 30 (Dover Publications), 46 top, 56 bottom (Dover Publications), 58, 65, 85 bottom, 91, 98 bottom (Dover Publications), 101, 106 (Dover Publications); Michael Holford: 13, 22 *Odin at the Waterfall by Henry Fuseli* (British Museum), 41 (British Museum), 88, 118, 120; Images Colour Library (Leeds and London): 21 left (National Gallery), 73 (Bibliothèque Nationale, Paris), 93, 95 top, 95 bottom *The Seventh Palace of Hell by Fay Pomerance* (Private Collection); Francis King: 148 top & bottom, 149 top & bottom; Kobal Collection: 48, 49 top, 64 top, 116, 141; London Features International: 144 top, 144 bottom (James Shive), 145 left (Swaine), 145 right; Mansell Collection: 31 bottom, 60 bottom, 104, 113 top & bottom; Mary Evans Picture Library: 31 top, 50, 54, 57, 61, 62, 66, 71, 72 bottom, 78 top, 78 bottom, 79, 89, 92 right, 97 bottom, 109, 110, 127 top & bottom (Harry Price Collection, University of London); Picturepoint – London: 26 bottom *Auto-da-Fé by P. Berruquete* (Prado Museum, Madrid), 27 *The Inquisition by E. Lucas* (Lazaro Galdeano Museum, Madrid), 28, 40 top, 74, 75 top & bottom *Murals showing Basque Witches* (Basque Museum, Bayonne, France), 139 top; David Redfern: 142, 143 top, 143 bottom (David Ellis); Frank Spooner Pictures: 132, 133 top & bottom (photos Patrick Aventurier); H. Roger-Viollet: 111 top & bottom.

B. Berg